Heart 2 Heart Teaching:
Building an Enduring Legacy in the Lives of Our Kids
(1st Edition)

by
Steve Woolf

Heart 2 Heart Teaching: Building An Enduring Legacy In The Lives Of Our Kids

DEDICATION

This book is a labor of love dedicated to my wife, Kellie, my sons, Stephen, Jake, Tanner, and Chris, and all of the educators and parents who live, love, learn, and leave a legacy with the little time we are given here on earth. Thank you for making your life count!

IN PRAISE OF HEART 2 HEART TEACHING (1st Edition)

Steve Woolf's Heart 2 Heart Teaching: Building an Enduring Legacy in the Lives of Our Kids is a warm, wise, wonderful little gem of a book. Steve takes just ten readable chapters to present the distilled essence of what it can mean to "kids" when caring teachers understand and act on authentically-connected, "heart to heart teaching."

Steve Woolf is a masterful story teller, and the stories he features in "Heart to Heart Teaching" are about real people; they are vivid, sometimes heartbreakingly tragic, but inevitably filled with informed insight—the kind of reflective thought that will give anyone who cares about human welfare and effective teaching useful insights about how to teach: not just "competently", but memorably.

Heart 2 Heart Teaching should be meaningful for a wide audience. Parents, pre-service teachers, practitioners and professors will find grounding principles and values in Steve's work that will serve them—and their kids—as they have a right to be served.

Dr. George Crawford
Professor of Education Leadership
University of Kansas (retired)

"Heart 2 Heart Teaching: Building an Enduring Legacy in the Lives of Our Kids" can be described as inspired. Steve created a book that helps people understand what students need to

truly be successful in their educational lives, adults who "get it" and truly care for their students. His ability to draw you in, as a storyteller, is outstanding. The book is a great read and you will find yourself wanting to read it multiple times. "Heart 2 Heart Teaching" puts our education system in a focused light to display a true picture of what is needed for our students. This book is for everyone from the novice teacher, administrators, to parents. You can't go wrong reading Steve's amazing book."

Dr. Michelle Carney-Ray, Ed.D.
Principal/Special Education Director and Anti-Bullying Coordinator,
Margate City Schools, New Jersey

"Heart 2 Heart Teaching" is just that: a great message from the heart of an excellent educator to another educator. Steve Woolf passionately shares how his values have been shaped by family, friends, and educators throughout his life to become one who has positively changed lives and impacted futures through the field of education. You will be inspired by the stories, engaged by the conversational You Tube videos at the end of each chapter, and you will be emotionally moved by stories shared throughout this book. This book exudes Steve's loving personality and I will share Steve's powerful message with new teachers who have accepted the call as a reminder of why they

became educators in the midst of the most challenging, yet opportunistic time in our profession."
Be Great,

Dwight Carter - High School Principal, 2010 Jostens Renaissance Hall of Fame Educator, 2013 NASSP Digital Principal of the Year, 2014 Bammy Award Winning Secondary Principal of the Year

In "Heart 2 Heart Teaching," Steve Woolf has captured a collection of must read compelling stories that teachers, parents, and all who love humanity will embrace with head nodding agreement that this narrative captures how all children should be treated. Steve has transferred his inspiring and well known stories of real life experiences in education into a book that reads like the best motivational speech on loving and teaching kids that one could ever want to hear. As one of the most respected educational leaders in the country, Steve Woolf's life changing knowledge on changing the lives of kids may now be enjoyed by all via this fun, can't put it down book. Like other great life changing books, the reader will want to share the message with others and reread the stories time and time again. This is a must read."

Dr. Mike Neal -
Assistant Dean of the School of Education at the University of Kansas

ABOUT THE AUTHOR

Steve Woolf is a nationally recognized leader, speaker, and now author on school climate and culture as well as teaching from the heart—to the heart in building connections with students. Steve also serves as a superintendent of schools and was a middle school principal for eighteen years before that. He started his career in education as a teacher in Topeka, Kansas.

Steve is married to his lovely wife, Kellie, and has four sons—Stephen, Jake, Tanner, and Chris. In addition to being a middle school principal and superintendent for the past 26 years, Steve is sought after to speak across the nation on issues dealing with leadership, student connection and motivation, and preparing our schools to ready our students to pursue their passions.

Steve was named the Kansas Middle School Principal of the Year in 1994 after his third year of being a principal. He was awarded the $25,000 Milken National Educator Award in 1995. In 2002, Steve was inducted into the Jostens Renaissance Educators Hall of Fame. In 2013 Steve received the Kansas Excellence in Conservation and Environmental Education Award. Steve is currently the superintendent of schools in Erie, Kansas.

In addition to time spent with his family, school, and speaking engagements, Steve is often involved with "Mountain Man" reenactments and

Scottish Heavy Throwing Events. He also builds community gardens and loves to be engaged in building projects around his home. Steve has also acted in "Focus On The Family" segments, commercials, and film.

Oh ... and Steve also tied for first place at his 1st grade field day competition in the 30-yard dash. Honest ... he has the ribbon and everything. ☺

Preface

Passion. I've never known anyone who was great at anything who wasn't also passionate about what they did. Since I believe it is absolutely essential we have great teachers teaching our kids, I also believe that passion is a key. If you talk to great, passionate educators, you will discover something about nearly all of them—they are relationship driven. There are so many "how to" books available that focus on classroom practice that never quite get to the heart of who we are as educators. What we do is so much more than a science. It is an art—an act of love from us to our students. My hope is that the combination of "story" and "research" will provide an impetus toward teaching from the heart, to the heart.

I speak throughout the nation, and I am approached at every event by people who want the content of my talks in book form. Whether or not you have heard me speak, it is my hope that this book will spread "Heart 2 Heart Teaching" throughout the world. I believe it will serve as a constant reminder of WHY we do what we do. There are plenty of books on the WHAT and the HOW. The heart of what we do is in the question "Why?"

I am not a professional author. What you will get in this book is simply a heartfelt account of what has proven to be true in my 28+ years as a teacher, principal, and superintendent. This is written for those who reach deep down to give their all to the people in their lives—students, faculty, friends, and family. It doesn't matter what position you may hold in education or if you do not have a position in education but just love kids. This is written for those interested in the power of connection, relationship, and the heart.

Each chapter carries a different aspect of "Heart 2 Heart Teaching" and usually a different piece or pieces of supporting research with stories to bring them to life. You may have difficulty remembering the exact research, but you will not likely have a problem remembering the stories. They bring life to the research and why we do what we do. It is also shines a light on what happens if connections and relationships are not a part of our schools. I would love to see every pre-practice education student in our colleges read this. It would help them focus up front on the "Why" of what we do.

A unique aspect of this book is at the end of each chapter you will find a QAR code and a web address to a short talk by me on the "Heart 2 Heart Teacher" You Tube Channel. This allows me to go into a little more depth on what I have written and allow you to hear "the voice" in which the book was written.

Some of these are shot in one of my favorite places—my kitchen—and there are other locations as well that provide a setting to the chapters. There is also a blog to support the concepts introduced in this book and to communicate with other Heart 2 Heart Teachers: **www.heart2heartteacher.com**. I hope you enjoy the opportunity to develop the "Tribe" of Heart 2 Heart Teachers throughout the world.

As I stated earlier, "How to" or "What to" books are in abundance for educators. Everyone is glad to tell us how to teach and what to teach whether they know anything about it or not. I find that most of these books are written by people who have not stepped into a Pre-K—12 school in years. There are authors out there who write on this subject, but I have found very few that focus on this area.

One of the great ones, who has taken on this endeavor as an author, speaker, and passionate educator, has blessed me by writing the Foreword to this book. I appreciate Angela Maiers setting the stage for your journey through the book. It is my hope and Angela's hope and the hope of all of the "Heart To Heart Teachers" out there that this helps fill a gap in the "Why" of what we do and fuels the passion for educators throughout the world.

The following is a short "Welcome to Heart 2 Heart Teaching" video. Enjoy!
http://youtu.be/9yHaHuBUxT4

FOREWORD

by Angela Maiers
Passionate Educator, International Speaker and Renowned Author of "Classroom Habitudes" and "The Passion Driven Classroom"

A teacher will see hundreds or even thousands of faces pass through the classroom during a career. One can usually tell the best teachers by their ability to look into any student's eyes and assess and address the student's well-being and development. For some it comes naturally, and for others it takes a gradual opening of the heart and mind. Whatever your place on this path of compassionate action, *Heart To Heart Teaching* will both inspire and inform your work in developing young minds.

In this book, Steve draws upon his decades of service as an educator to coach us on how to profoundly impact students' lives. The stories he shares relate a deep experience of transforming others. Equally convincing was Steve's use of research to cement the outcomes of his own experience. Teaching has become increasingly evidence-based, and *Heart 2 Heart Teaching* offers the science behind the stories—the data behind the day-to-day. I can think of no better way to assess educational research than through the lens of such a veteran teacher and administrator.

If you know Steve personally, you won't be surprised how his values emanate from these pages. His writing, much like his work as an educator, is driven by an attention to relationships, empathy, and joy. These are the foundation of having importance in students' lives: no matter how many mistakes one makes, the driving force for serving others is your beliefs and strength of mission.

As a teaching corps, we educators grow stronger by sharing our experiences. Every school, every student, presents unique challenges. Within *Heart 2 Heart Teaching*, Steve turns his individual stories into universal principles. When we open our ears and hearts to his message, it is bound to affect the way we treat people around us. I have been inspired by Steve's work, and I'm certain the same will hold true for you.

Chapter 1 - WHY?

"Do you really care, or is it just your job?"
-Jodi, one of Steve's Students

Why is it that some teachers seem to be able to get kids to do anything and some get near to nothing? I've seen coaches who had players who would run through a brick wall for them and other coaches who struggled to get kids to show up for practice. There are teachers I have been blessed to watch where kids simply do not want to leave their classrooms. If there is an evening study session, they are there. If that teacher's classroom is "open" during lunch, students are there. If there is a project that needs worked on that goes on after school, these teachers almost have to run kids away from school because they would stay as long as that teacher stayed. You have likely had these teachers in your life, and you may not have even stopped to consider why they were able to do that. I know that was the case for me until I realized that I was copying what they had done for me in my own career with kids. I am sure they didn't realize it at the time, but they were building their legacy in me.

Dr. John Hattie (2008) has done the most exhaustive meta-analysis in education considering what works best in the classroom. There are things we have done in education that have actually had detrimental effects, things that really didn't matter one way or another, and things that truly make a difference in the classroom. One of his discoveries was that "teacher-student relationships fostered" was one of the top classroom practices that facilitates student learning. The great thing about this is it is free—it just costs an investment of heart and time. More than "Application of Knowledge (1.30 years of growth projected)" and use of "Literacy Strategies (1.22 years of growth)" is "Student Teacher Relationship (1.44 years of growth)."[1]

"Story" is a powerful learning tool, maybe THE most powerful tool we have in our arsenal as teachers. Sometimes we remember research, theorems, postulates, and laws, but when put into a story, the likelihood of remembering these grows exponentially depending on the power of the story to move us. When a story moves us to deep thought, laughter or tears, our brain releases endorphins that sear them into our memory.

This book is a journey of research and story that addresses the amazing power that we possess to mold the minds and hearts of our students. We will look at those "blinding flashes of the obvious" that you and I know to be true, yet we often forget because we are so drawn into and consumed by the minutia that pulls our attention elsewhere.

---

[1] Hattie, John (2009). *Visible Learning; a synthesis of over 800 meta-analyses relating to achievement* (London; Routledge, 2009)

As you read the stories that accompany the research and ideas in this book, I believe your own stories, even ones buried in your subconscious, will come flooding back. These are the stories that support the truth of who you are as an educator, parent, or simply a caring human being. Chances are good that you will be able to take the stories out of this book and replace them with your own to support the ideas and concepts that lie within these pages.

Dr. Al Wilson would absolutely NOT remember me as a student at Kansas State University. I was about as unspectacular as a student as one can get in college. Looking back, I cannot remember one relationship or connection I built with a professor at KSU. That may explain my "unspectacular" academic performance … yes, let's blame it on that. With that in mind, Dr. Wilson said something in our "Principalship" class one evening that moved me and impacted just about every area in my life as an educator, parent, husband, and friend.

Dr. Wilson told us to remember to use the "6 to 1 Concept"—six positives to one negative. Whenever we visited with our staff and students, we should always work to say six positive things to one corrective or perceived negative thing. I'm not sure I heard anything else he said that night because his "621" concept enveloped any cognitive activity that was happening.

At the time I was working as a residence hall director at KSU to pay my way through my Master's Degree program. I had a staff of Resident Assistants as well as a residence hall full of students. Most of these residents were either graduate students who were older than I was, foreign students, or members of KSU's men's basketball team.

I thought I was doing a pretty good job implementing what Dr. Wilson had talked about already, but now it was going to be purposeful. Now I was going to be able to use that as a tool to make a deeper impact in the lives of those I encountered.

Looking back now at the impact that piece of advice had on my career and relationships, I can see that it wasn't the magical formula of "6 to 1" that made the real difference. It was the willingness to open myself up to genuinely love and care for my students and staff—to dare to share my whole heart so that they would know they are special to me and that I want the very best for them.

It was at that time it hit me that I did not have to lead from a position of power. I could lead from a position of relationship and connection like the most powerful educators in my life did for me. Students and staff would begin to share with me that they would follow me because they knew I cared deeply and that they simply wanted to please me. That seemed to me to be a much better concept for leading than to have people follow to avoid punishment.

The comedian, actor, and musician Steve Martin cracks me up. I love to laugh, and he definitely has the ability to get me rolling. In his role as a corporate leader in the movie "Baby Mama" he "rewards" Tina Fey's character with "five minutes of uninterrupted eye contact." Five minutes of uninterrupted eye contact … I'm not sure there could be something much more uncomfortable for me to experience. I'm not sure I could do that with my wife, let alone anyone else. I found the scene on You Tube, and it reminded me that while leading from relationship is highly effective, if the connection is one-sided or actually over the line of appropriateness, it is actually counter productive.[2]

The most recent example of powerful connection that comes to mind is of a "retired" teacher at Central Plains High School in central Kansas named Robert John. Robert retired from a career teaching at Quivira Heights High School, but he could not stay away. He still teaches part time but makes a full time difference in the lives of the students he serves.

I first met Robert when I was a sophomore at Claflin High School. He would not remember that

---

[2] Baby Mama (2008). https://www.youtube.com/watch?v=IMSd1IbxmFA.

meeting, but I most certainly do. As I stated, he was a teacher in the neighboring high school, Quivira Heights High School, and they organized town team basketball at that high school. I heard that they may need an extra player, and I would go anywhere for a game of basketball. Robert welcomed me with open arms, talked to me, took an interest in me and made me feel I was of value. My dad was a guidance counselor in the same school in which Robert taught, and the next day he told my dad I was a pretty good basketball player. (He may have exaggerated a little). I was hooked. I knew that if that guy were my teacher, I would run through a wall for him.

Later in my life, I became superintendent of the school district in which Robert taught, and Robert became one of my son's physics teacher. The night before each physics test, Robert would invite all of his students to his home to review for the test. The review involved milk and chocolate chip cookies made by Robert's lovely wife.

Kids felt very comfortable there. They felt wanted and valued. Would it surprise any of you that the conversation often drifted off of physics and toward deeper conversations that were life builders? Robert John was my son's favorite teacher.

To take Robert's ability to open up and create connections further, my youngest son did not have Robert as a teacher at all during his high school career. When I asked him who his favorite high school teacher was, he didn't hesitate with his answer—Mr. John. Just the interactions with Mr. John in the hallway, at activities, and at ballgames moved my son. He wanted to be better to please Mr. John, and Mr. John was not ever his teacher. Mr. John knew my sons. Robert John cared about my sons.

Every summer kids look forward to going on a Robert John led trip to Washington D.C. While the trip is memorable and educational, it isn't hard to tell that one of the greatest benefits of the trip to the kids is time with Mr. John. I don't know if Robert John really "gets" the impact he has on kids, but I know it when I see it, and when I see the power of teaching from the heart - to the heart, it is amazingly obvious.

The rest of this book will look at some powerful research, great teachers, moving stories, blinding-flashes-of-the-obvious, and you as we journey into the power of teaching from the heart – to the heart. My hope is that you will learn as much as possible about the problems that occur when we do not purposefully harness the power of relationship. I also hope you will see what happens when the full power of relationship is engaged. Our lives, along with the lives of our students, our staff, and our families, will never be the same.

Much of what I learned in this area came from the greats: Stephen Covey, Malcolm Gladwell, Paul

Fitzgerald, Daniel Pink, Ruby Payne, John Lynch, Kevin Honeycutt, Larry Biddle, and Brene' Brown.

Other amazing life lessons came from my wonderful wife, Kellie, my dad, my mom, my amazing sons, and all of the students and educators that I have been blessed to have as a part of my life over the years. When I tied all of our research, practice, experiences, and stories to my 50+ years of living, 28 years as an educator, 27 years as a Dad, 4 years as a teacher, 18 years as a middle school principal, and 6 years as a superintendent, the pieces started to fall into place.

As I stated in the Preface, at the end of each chapter there will be a web address and a QAR code that will take you to my "Heart 2 Heart Teaching" You Tube channel where I will take a few minutes to share a little extra and sometimes go a little deeper about what you have just read. Most of the videos will come right from my kitchen. Yep ... my kitchen. I'll explain why in the videos. One thing you may notice in the You Tube videos is that during the course of getting around to filming for all of the chapters of this book I lost 70 pounds from the first video we shot to the last. That is a whole other story.

Check out the Chapter 1 "Post Chapter Video" on You Tube at the following:
http://youtu.be/9NpblJAwuhU

Chapter 2 - 26,280 Days

"A company is stronger if it is bound by love rather than by fear."
-Herb Kelleher, CEO Southwest Airlines

"In this life we cannot do great things. We can only do small things with great love."
-Mother Teresa

"Your past is important, but it is not nearly as important to your present as the way you see your future."
-Tony Campolo, author, sociologist, minister, and professor emeritus at Eastern University

As I begin to write this book I am 18,530 days old. Having been born in 1962 and being a male, I have read that I can expect to live to be 72 years old or 26,280 days if I can avoid heart attacks, strokes, cancer, or big trucks. I hit another milestone birthday this year ... forty-ten years old. That's right ... a half-century. Fifty doesn't really bother me, and 40 didn't really bother me.

The age that hit me right in the middle of the forehead was 36. I did the math, and as it turns out, 36 is half of 72. Half of my life was gone and no amount of Bill Gates money would buy one day back! Up until that time, I did not really think of my life as being finite. When that reality struck, it made a difference in how I wanted to spend the time I had left on this Earth.

I knew at the age of "twenty-sixteen" that I wanted my life to count but wondered if it really did. My personal mission statement at the time of "Living, loving, learning, and leaving a legacy while keeping my priorities of being a husband, daddy, and educator" was a driving force for me, and it all pointed back to me simply being passionate about people.

Striving to build connection, to build relationships, had been a powerful tool for me as I journeyed through life thus far, and it hit me that I could truly touch the future well beyond my years here on earth if I would continue to give in to what I believe is natural for man and build strong, loving relationships whenever possible. The people I saw who invested their life in anything other than the lives of people always seemed dissatisfied and wanting for more.

To make that investment in my life and into the lives of the thousands of kids I have the pleasure of serving as an educator, I realized I needed to be willing to get out of the box and dare to love and connect with people in a way that usually doesn't happen unless you purposefully look to do so. To actually make powerful differences in the lives of all of these students, staff, and others around me would require me to do two things—think differently and act differently.

Tony Campollo shared a study he was involved with from the early 1980s that may be the single most powerful study I have ever heard. It changed my life. They gathered 50 people into one room to ask them the question "What would you do different if you could live life again?" The study had two powerful components to it.

The first was that all of the participants in the study were 95 years old or older. Since this study was conducted in the early '80s we can surmise that most were born in 1885 or before. When they were born, there weren't more than 200 miles of paved roads in the United States. They saw the advent of automobiles, the telephone, electricity in homes, electric light, the splitting of the atom, radio, television, and flight. They lived through World War I, World War II, the Korean War, and Vietnam. They lived through the Dust Bowl, The Great Depression, the "Hippie Movement," and experienced the wonder that was the "Yuppie."

The second powerful aspect of this study is truly amazing. They ALL agreed on three things they would do different if they could live life over again. If you have ever spent time with folks that fall near this age demographic, then you know that they have opinions ... strong opinions. At age 95, they feel they have earned the right not to have to back off of their position at this point in their lives.

Knowing this and then knowing that they ALL AGREED on the three things that they would do different is powerful. If you can't learn from fifty 95-year-old men and women who have experienced all they have experienced in life and agree on what they would do if they could live life again, then you can't learn from anybody.

The first thing they would do is they would "reflect more." This does not mean they would make themselves shiny. This means that this group of 95-year-old men and women would take the special moments that happen throughout our lives, rework them in their mind, and think about them regularly. What they understand at the age of 95 is this: Most of the people they cared about, impacted them, or traveled the journey of life with them are gone. The only thing they have left of these people that have been a part of their lives is the memories that they built together.

Cognitively, we know that if people do not continue to re-work memories and thoughts in their minds, they get pushed to the far recesses where, for all practical purposes, they disappear.[3] Word cues can help bring back those memories, but if they have not been brought up on a semi-regular basis (studies continue on how regular this needs to be), these jewels are lost. Cognitively, it seems to be true that if you don't use it, you lose it.

The second thing the 95-year-old crew would

---

[3] Craik, F.I.M., & McDowd, J.M. (1987). Age-differences in recall and recognition. *Journal of Experimental Psychology: Learning, Memory and Cognition,* 13, 474-479.

do different if they could live life again is Take More Risks! They would step outside the box and color outside the lines much more than they did. As they look back, they realize that life gave them some amazing opportunities they did not grab. If they could live life again, they would, to borrow a slogan from Nike, "Just do it!"

Life gave the 95-year-old crew and us who live today amazing opportunities to make differences in the world and the people that inhabit it. Many times this requires stepping outside of the box. Another way to say this would be by borrowing an advertising phrase from Apple when they urged us to "Think Different."

A prime example of thinking outside of the box and taking risk is Herb Kelleher. Herb Kelleher was the co-founder, CEO, and Head Cheerleader for Southwest Airlines. Herb and a friend, Rollin King, developed the business plan for Southwest Airlines on a cocktail napkin at a restaurant.

Then he did something spectacular ... he acted on it! They decided that they were going to "color outside of the lines" in just about everything they did in building the airline. Every other airline was using a hub system to get people from point A to point B to point C. Herb decided that going from point A to point C, without going to point B, and doing it on time at a lower price seemed like a better idea. Instead of going through the hardship of assigning everyone a seat, he simply said, "first come – first served" and got the plane in the air. He grabbed onto a "blinding flash of the obvious" that his planes made more money when they were in the air than when they were sitting at the gate. He engaged everyone—pilots, flight attendants, and anyone else that was available that worked their airline—to clean the plane up, turn it around, and get it in the air again.

Herb understood the power of "play." He realized life is short so he played hard in and out of work. If you have ever flown on a Southwest flight, then you know that, chances are, you are going to hear something funny or different when they are giving the safety instructions. The employees dare to laugh as they work hard. In fact, it is difficult to know whether they are working or playing at times.

In 1992, the CEO of Stevens Aviation called Southwest Airlines out on using the slogan "Just Plane Smart" because Stevens Aviation had come up with the slogan and was already using it. In normal situations, the lawsuits would come quickly at great cost to both companies. Instead, realizing the great cost involved with litigation, the two CEO's thought outside of the box and did something completely different that did not involve any attorneys. They arm-wrestled for it!

They titled the arm wrestling duel "The Malice In Dallas." The winner got to use the slogan and the loser had to donate to the winner's charity of choice. Southwest Airlines ran with it, and the positive publicity, as well as the wonderful, fun feeling inside the companies, was rampant. National and local media covered the event like it was really an athletic competition.[4]

Southwest Airlines made "Rocky" themed promotional videos for their staff to watch and get excited about the event. The CEO of Stevens Aviation was a gentleman who worked out with weights and was in very good shape for the event. Kelleher was not. Herb Kelleher is a chain smoking, hard drinking CEO. His work out videos were hilarious with him always smoking while "working out" and lifting jugs of Wild Turkey instead of weights. There was little doubt of the outcome of the event.

In the end the event was spectacular for both companies. Kelleher lost and both agreed to donate to the other's cause anyway. The Cleveland Ronald McDonald House and the Muscular Dystrophy Association were winners and Southwest Airlines was a major winner with more free publicity than they could afford otherwise. In the end, Stevens Aviation, allowed Southwest Airlines to "use our slogan" anyway.

Taking the risk of being different from everyone else in the airline industry is the main staple of success for Southwest Airlines. The "drones" of society do not like to see others step

---

[4] As The Planes Turn. "Southwest Airlines "Malice in Dallas" Part Five." http://www.youtube.com/watch?v=H_sXAdUNFnc

outside the ordinary to succeed. Southwest Airlines had to fight off lawsuits from many other airlines that no longer exist because they took risks to succeed after the deregulation of pricing in the airline industry. In the end, the risk of thinking differently and behaving differently is what makes them great.

The third thing the 95-year-olds would do different is invest their time in more things that will last long after they are gone. They wanted their lives to count for something. They wanted the world to be a better place because they had walked upon it. Just as Boy Scouts who go camping are required to "Leave the campsite better than you found it," these nonagenarians would focus on creating a lasting legacy if they could do it all over again.

There are the obvious people who have done this in our world – Gandhi, Martin Luther King, jr., Edison, Jefferson, Eisenhower, Mother Theresa to name a few, but behind all of these people were teachers, neighbors, friends, and family who moved in their lives to help them become the world changers they were. There were teachers who touched their lives, neighbors who showed some kindness, and family members who supported, motivated, and invested in them one way or another.

The people who changed the world did not start out with that goal in mind. They did one small thing after another that added up to great events that changed the world.

President General Dwight D. Eisenhower started his life learning to work hard in the central Kansas town of Abilene. The teachers and coaches there played a huge part in molding the man who led our country to victory in World War II and made many essential decisions as President of the United States that ranged from supporting the space program and the beginning of civil rights support to starting the Interstate Highway System in the U.S. He definitely left the campground better than he found it.

Eisenhower's reflections of a life well led, the risks he had to take as the leader of the combined forces in WWII, and his time as President of the United States prove he made a difference that continues long after he breathed his last on this earth in 1969. Eisenhower lived past his 26,280 days by a few years—he died at age 79, but his life's work other than the written reflection of that work was done in the first 72 years.

The others mentioned have similar stories that range from the thousands of times Edison had to try to find the right filament to create the light bulb to Mother Theresa living the example of doing small things with great love. These people exemplified all three of the things the 95-year-olds said they would do if they could live life again. They were the culmination of the connections they made throughout their lives. The connections they made in youth were built upon by connections they continued to make as they shared their talents with the world. My dear friend, Kevin Honeycutt, would say, "They lived their life out loud!"

As an educator or a parent, the chance to live, love, and learn out loud is an awesome gift to give to our kids and a responsibility that is daunting to some. We have been given the amazing gift of time—hopefully at least 26,280 days. I recently overheard a teacher talking about not being able to wait until the weekend ... and it was only Tuesday. There was a lot of time to make a difference in the lives of her students, her family, and all of the people whose paths she crossed before Friday. Monday–Friday ... life is lived in the "dash."

I learned this from the man who made the biggest difference in my life—my dad. He was a guidance counselor, but more importantly, he was my best friend, cheerleader, personal coach, and father. Everything I accomplished, I did to make him proud. When he passed away, it was a huge loss, but his legacy lives on through me and all the other lives he touched as a counselor, coach, dad, and friend.

At his funeral and visitation, so many shared with me the difference my Dad made in their lives as an educator. Many shared that they owed who they were to the love and guidance he gave. I recently visited him at his grave in the tiny town of

Claflin, KS. I noticed the dates on the tombstone: October 30, 1935–April 15, 2012. I stared at the dash between 1935 and April. That is where his life was lived as a husband, daddy, and an educator. He lived life in the dash, and although he would be considered a quiet man, he lived life out loud!

Helping our students to live a life of passion, creativity, and commitment to something great is a clear goal for us as educators and parents. To do that is much easier if we are modeling that behavior. Establishing that relationship that allows us to reach and teach deeply is key. People can see passion, creativity, and commitment. Without relationship, it is difficult to know the reason for these important attributes in the life of the educator, parent, or friend. That requires openness, honesty, and vulnerability. It requires the real you to shine through.

There was a method to Herb Kelleher's madness. His was a desire to be open, creative, and passionate—to live his life out loud. In the end, he changed the way airlines think and act. Through his risks, he made a difference in the airline industry that will last long after he is gone.

I've watched great teachers and I've wondered, "Is there a method to their madness?" The answer is "Yes!" There was passion for learning and a love for their students.

Check out the Chapter 2 "Post Chapter

Video" on You Tube at the following:
http://youtu.be/1BjJmm3wVpU

Chapter 3 - Brave Heart

"Unless you can know fear, it is impossible to be brave". – Steve Woolf

"What we do in life, echoes in eternity" – Maximus "Gladiator"

If you have ever spent much time with kids at our schools in this nation, you have no doubt run into some kids who are unbelievably brave. Many of the brave people I run into in my life have been our students. They come to us from such varied backgrounds. In one school you may have students who are from affluent, supportive families who never want for anything sitting next to students who are from homes where poverty, alcoholism, and abuse run rampant. We usually end up making the mistake of expecting these two examples of kids to behave and respond the same. That expectation would be a huge mistake.

President Theodore Roosevelt gave a speech at the Sorbonne in Paris, France on April 23, 1910 that spoke to bravery well. He said, *"It is not the critic who counts; not the man who points out how the strong man stumbles, or where the doer of deeds could have done them better. The credit belongs to the man who is actually in the arena, whose face is marred by dust and sweat and blood; who strives valiantly; who errs, who comes short again and again, because there is no effort without error and shortcoming; but who does actually strive to do the deeds; who knows great enthusiasms, the great devotions; who spends himself in a worthy cause; who at the best knows in the end the triumph of high achievement, and who at the worst, if he fails, at least fails while daring greatly, so that his place shall never be with those cold and timid souls who neither know victory nor defeat."*

For many of our kids, every day of their existence they "step into the arena." It isn't just at school that they "step into the arena," but it is from the moment they rise to deal with the hand they have been dealt at home until the moment they find a place to sleep for the night.

Knowing this, it is our responsibility to cheer them on. It seems that most of our society predicts failure for those who are stuck in poverty and very adverse circumstance. The kids who dare to "step into the arena" understand that they are the underdog. They understand that there may be "booing" and an expectation to fail based on who they are when they walk into the arena. They understand that the people who built the "arena" tend to cheer those on that are most like the builders of the arena, yet they walk into the arena afraid … and in spite of their fear, they are brave.

These kids have come to the realization that you can choose courage or you can choose comfort, but you cannot have both. Being brave takes us out of our comfort zone and is vital to break through life's circumstances. As adults and educators, it is our responsibility to prepare our kids for the "arena." This involves having the courage to develop a relationship with the kid … often not comfortable for either. It requires us to be their cheerleader, their confidant, their coach, and their teacher.

I love Brene' Brown's description of stories as "data with a soul." This book has been peppered with "data with a soul." I do this because I have discovered, as our ancestors who wrote fables, legends, and parables before us, that this type of "data" not only goes into the mind, but it moves to the heart. With that in mind, I would like to share some "data" on Shaun.

Shaun was a seventh grade young man who had managed to achieve "frequent flier" status in our middle school office. He sought attention and received it the easy way—poor behavior. We knew that life was tough for this young man. If you have ever driven south out of Colorado Springs, CO on I-25 toward Pueblo you would notice a KOA Campground just to the east of the highway in the Fort Carson vicinity. That is where Shaun lived in a four door sedan with a dad who looked like a Hell's Angel, a mom who was beaten down by his dad, and a third grade brother. Let me repeat that—he lived in a car. We had been concerned for the social, mental, and physical well being of this kid throughout his seventh grade year.

Shaun barely made it through his seventh grade year academically and now we were starting his eighth grade year. My assistant principal and I made our normal beginning of the year presentations to the students, and one of the things we presented to the kids was our plan to reward, recognize, respect, and reinforce academic achievement, great attitudes, and positive actions as much or more than what has been typically reserved for athletic achievement. Some of what we called the "4 R's" involved earning different levels of cards that came with different extra prizes and privileges. In this school, it worked amazingly well and now, eighteen years later, the program is still making a difference in students' lives, but I digress.

Shaun came up to my assistant principal and me after our presentation and informed us that he was going to earn one of the achievement cards. We smiled and sent Shaun on his way. We knew there was no way the Shaun we knew from the year before was going to earn a reward card. The lowest level card required a 3.0 GPA (or a 0.5 increase in GPA over the previous quarter), no discipline referrals, no more than one tardy, and no unexcused absences.

As we talked and laughed a little about Shaun coming up and announcing to us that he was going to earn a card, we thought "Why not?" To do this we were going to have to work to put success in his path. One of the things we knew intuitively and from research is that students involved in activities tend to perform substantially better than students not involved in activities. We needed to get Shaun involved.

With the start of each school year brings football. We knew that Shaun didn't have the physical examination that he would have to have to compete. He would have no football shoes to wear, and we knew he would have no ride home from practice to the KOA Campground miles away. We worked to set all of these things up and then we approached him. "Shaun, would you like to play football?" He replied, "OK." It was on!

Shaun had an amazing football season. He was a big, blonde, shaggy haired kid who absolutely excelled at football. By the end of the nine-week grade period, which also coincided with the end of the football season, Shaun had a 3.0 GPA, no discipline referrals, no tardies, and no unexcused absences. He had earned his card! He was so proud at our first Academic Pep Assembly when he was able to come forward and get his card. Most of the students and many staff members were a little slack jawed when they saw Shaun rise to go receive his just reward. However, we did have a problem … football was over.

"Hey, Shaun! Want to be on the wrestling team?"

"OK."

As administrators, we must supervise all of our activities. My assistant principal and I were dividing up duties between the two sports that coincided— wrestling and volleyball. While I love volleyball, this was before the "rally scoring system" was brought in and it took forever for some of our middle school volleyball games to end. With that in mind, I volunteered for wrestling. I didn't know much about wrestling, but I could cheer loudly.

Shaun was our heavy weight wrestler. As it turned out, he was also a great wrestler. I couldn't help but marvel at this young man who entered the arena every match with all of the pressures that come with the life he led. He had the pressure of living in a car. He had the pressure of living with a dad who was prone to abuse. He had the pressure of trying to protect his mom and his brother from his dad. He had the pressure of trying to make sure he had something clean to wear to school. He had the pressure of often times trying to find food to eat when they had run out. Now he had the pressure of being the last wrestler of every wrestling meet with the team's win or loss often falling to him. I like to joke that there is also the pressure of having to wear the "onesie" that wrestlers have to wear as a uniform to compete in, but I have since been corrected and informed it is called a singlet. I could see the stress on his face every time he stepped on the mat. It tied my empathetic gut in a knot as well.

Shaun and I developed a ritual after every one of his matches. I am sure that as you pictured Shaun in your mind at the wrestling matches, you did not picture Shaun's parents in attendance. You would be correct. They never did attend a football game, wrestling match, or a track meet (the spring sport he participated in that year). I thought I would have to comfort him after losing a match, but I never did have to. He won every match! Our ritual involved me running to the edge of the mat after he won, putting my arm around his neck in a hug (and doing a little "head butt" to "be men about it"), and then me saying "Shaun, I'm so proud of you!" His response was always the same as well … "Thank you, Sir." He learned "sir" in football that year.

It was the second to the last match of the year and Shaun was up against another undefeated wrestler. There was a large crowd that was loud and going a little nuts. It looked as though there were going to be a couple of wrestling matches in the crowd at one point, and now the win or loss for the team came down to the heavyweight match between Shaun and the other undefeated boy.

The match was back and forth, and Shaun was behind until the last few seconds when he got a reverse and pinned his opponent. The crowd went nuts! The other team's crowd was very upset that it was called a pin, and our home crowd was ecstatic. I had to immediately move through the crowd to keep fights from breaking out and work everyone out of the gym. I then worked my way home.

The next morning bright and early I was at my principal's desk working, and I looked up and flinched a little in surprise as Shaun was standing in my doorway. He had worked his way right past the secretaries and was standing there a little misty-eyed. I greeted him and then asked what he was up to. He replied with a question, "Why weren't you at my match last night?"

I responded, "Shaun, I was there! I'm hoarse this morning from screaming so loudly. Way to kick some butt!!"

Tears then started to roll down Shaun's face and he asked, "Why didn't you come down on the mat afterwards?"

My heart sank. Although I had an excuse, it was not a good one. I apologized and gushed over how well he was doing, but that didn't take the place of the moment that he was looking forward to after the match.

Shaun had one match left that season, and I raced down to the mat after he won and gave him a huge hug and "head bonk." That was the reward, recognition, respect, and reinforcement he was looking for. Shaun yearned for the same things we all want: love, respect, and connection! He hungered for the meaningful connection that relationship can bring to a young man in dire circumstances. Was he afraid to enter the arena? You bet he was. Was he brave? Absolutely!

He was willing to risk it all for the chance of Connection. The only way Shaun saw that he was going to have this chance to connect was to step into the arena and take advantage of the success that caring educators put in his path. The educators worked hard to create a path that did not allow him to dodge success as many kids manage to do.

They did this with love, the type of love that made Shaun want to check at the gate of the arena any shame he felt from the circumstances he was born into. He was shown that he was worthy of love and worthy of connection. He was worthy of success in the classroom arena, in the athletic arena, in the relationship arena, and in the arena of life.

Check out the Chapter 3 "Post Chapter Video" on You Tube at the following:

http://youtu.be/cCbi40dmiPk

Chapter 4 - Doughnuts, Vulnerability, & Ray

There's nothing like the feeling that you're really wanted!
– Charlie Brown

It's great to be wanted. I spent a few years not being wanted and this is better.
-Morgan Freeman

I can remember the little sixth grade boy, Ray, like it was yesterday. It is hard to believe it has been the number of years it has been since this incident occurred. Sometimes incidents happen in the life of an educator that define who you are and what you hope to accomplish in the lives of the children with whom we are trusted. Ray was the central character in this defining incident.

Ray and his twin sister were growing up in a Hispanic family in our largely Hispanic community. Ray, being semi-ornery, had built up quite a few "frequent flyer miles" in my office. The night before this incident had been tough for Ray. His dad had a particularly bad habit of drinking too much and then taking his anger out on Ray by beating him. The man that Ray loved more than any other man would usually use his tools to beat Ray. This time he used a wrench. One thing led to another and the Social Rehabilitation Service became involved and took Ray out of his home that night and put him into a foster home.

The next morning the SRS worker called me to let me in on the situation. My heart sank. It gets worse. I have this little ritual I perform as a principal for each of my students for their birthday. The ritual began when I started asking kids about how their birthday went the day after their birthday and occasionally I would have a student reply, "My parents forgot." Wow! Anyway, because of that I would take a Little Debbie cake, stick a candle in it, and sing my rendition of "Happy Birthday" poorly to them in front of their friends in the classroom. Students would act like they disliked this ritual and would often remind me well in advance not to sing to them on their birthday. It usually would go something like this, "My birthday is two months from today, and you had better NOT sing to me...2nd hour." ...And so 2nd hour it was! Guess whose birthday was that day. That's right—Ray's.

I continued doing "important middle school principal things" that morning and forgot to go talk to Ray's teacher and to Ray. When class started that morning, Ray's teacher had no clue what Ray had gone through the night before.

I'm sure you would not be surprised to know that Ray was not all that cooperative that morning. He had caused some sort of disruption and his teacher was having none of it. She marched him right down to the back hallway entrance to my office and with a firm grip on his arm, pushed him toward a chair in my office. She told me in front of Ray that he had caused a disruption in her class and that she was in no mood to put up with his shenanigans that day. You could hear the venom in her voice. The teacher then marched out of my office and back to her classroom.

There sat Ray. I could see and feel the combination of anger and shame emanating from him. It is amazing how much students can say to us without saying a word if we pay attention. I could tell he was preparing himself for the wrath of the principal that was about to befall him. I kept a semi-stern face, looked him in the eye, and said, "Get up and follow me."

Ray got up out of the chair and followed me through the office. I told my secretaries that we were leaving and that I would be back later. I think one of them replied "Good." I still don't know if that was "good" I was leaving or "good" I'll be back. Either way, secretaries pretty much run things in schools and they would survive without me. Ray and I marched down the back hallway and left the building. We crawled into my '83 Blazer (I splurged and moved up to an '88 Blazer recently) and headed on a route that took us past his home, his foster home, and on a path that I knew relatively well – the donut shop. I'm a big guy and I didn't get that way for nothing. ☺

I told Ray to get out of the car and follow me. He followed me to the counter and I ordered two old-fashioned doughnuts and a Diet-Pepsi. "Balance" … it didn't work. I asked Ray what he would like. He looked up at me and said, "I don't want nothin' from you." I let the lady who was waiting on us know that Ray would have two old-fashioned doughnuts and an orange juice. I took the tray of "goods" and sat at a table for two that happened to be in the path of the customer traffic coming in and out of the store. I put Ray's donuts and drink in front of him and looked at this 12 year-old boy who was in pain sitting across from me. I then used a semi-stern voice to say "Ray" and then I softened my voice to say "Happy Birthday, Ray." No one had remembered.

Ray broke into tears. Tears started to come to my eyes as well, but I managed, with a little "eye itching" to hold them back. Then I did something that I should do a lot more often than I do. After explaining to Ray that I knew what had happened to him and that I should have come to talk to him and his teacher, I said, "Ray,

I am so sorry I didn't talk to you and your teacher and I should have. Will you forgive me?" Ray wasn't exactly used to having his principal ask him for forgiveness and he uttered, "Uh, OK." I told the customers as they arrived that today was Ray's birthday and we were skipping school together. They would stop and supply the appropriate amount of well wishes for Ray on his birthday and Ray would shyly reply, "Thank you." Five minutes later he had gotten over his shyness and would announce in a rather loud voice and a big smile to customers arriving that "today is my birthday and I'm skipping school with the principal!"

We eventually made our way to my old car and drove back to the school. As we pulled into the parking lot, I asked Ray if he would do me a personal favor. Even though all of this was happening to him, would he behave the way he knew I wanted him to behave for the rest of the day? He replied, "Yes, sir." He kept his word and furthermore, although he had been a fairly "frequent flyer" before, I didn't see him again for a discipline referral for the remainder of the year.

I learned several lessons from my time with Ray that day. The first is to give yourself permission to step "outside of the box," take a risk, and do what is right for that child. When the teacher brought Ray to the office she wasn't thinking, "I hope he takes that boy out for some donuts and some love." She was thinking more in line with "Beat The Child!" You will never find this strategy in an educational textbook or manual. To be quite frank, it wouldn't work with every child. Many of the answers that we seek in dealing with children will not be found in an educational text and maybe not advocated by educational "experts," but they are the right thing to do at that time in that situation. Ray put me in a position where I had to step out of the box, and in doing that, he taught me a lesson.

Another valuable lesson I learned from Ray was to allow myself to be vulnerable with kids. Being real and truly allowing ourselves to be vulnerable, to be seen—really seen—for who we are, is the only way for connection and relationship to authentically occur. This is not only true for our connections, relationships, and interactions with kids, but it is true in all of our relationships. Ray would not trust me or work through his unearned shame, unless I allowed myself to be vulnerable to his acceptance or rejection and to be genuinely REAL.

This incident happened my second year as a middle school principal and since then I would like to tell you I have nailed it! That would be a lie. I am working hard to grow and love kids the way they deserve, but I have failed at this more times than I have time to write about. The bottom line is to keep trying. Keep working to embrace your vulnerability. Keep being real. If we keep growing as we work toward being more and more real, our interactions, connection, and relationship with those we come in contact with on a regular basis will grow despite our fears or rejection and sometimes shame.

I will delve into the concept of shame and its impact on students as well as society as a whole a little deeper in another chapter. Shame can absolutely paralyze relationships and growth for students, teachers, and anybody that comes under its great weight.

Check out the Chapter 4 "Post Chapter Video" on You Tube at the following:
http://youtu.be/7tqbLpwJlsY

Chapter 5 - Scratch My Kid
Behind His Ears

"You can judge a man's character by the way he treats the person with the least power in the room."
-Steve Woolf

"Students who are loved at home, come to school to learn, and student who aren't, come to school to be loved."
-Nicholas Ferroni, educator and historian

The following is an essay I wrote for my staff when I was a middle school principal over fifteen years ago. It was right before parent-teacher conferences, and I needed to share how important they are to loving, caring, and understanding our kids with their Whole Heart. The little boy of focus in the story is now a daddy, husband, construction/National Guard worker, and college student.

I had an opportunity to visit with my son, Jake's, teacher at a parent-teacher conference. My wife and I sat down, and the teacher gave a heavy sigh, looked at us, and said, "Tell me about Jake."
Now this kind of took me by surprise. I was looking forward to hearing from this teacher about Jake's performance the previous grade period.
Jake had looked forward to going to school each day up to this year and now he was coming home

saying, "My teacher doesn't like me." This is a pretty heavy statement coming from a 2nd grade boy.

While Jake did the activities he was supposed to in class and was performing pretty well academically, Jake was pretty "busy." I immediately told the teacher that she could probably blame this on genetics. With my reputation as a slightly hyper principal in another school, she understood. To be quite frank, I believe that the teacher really didn't care to have Jake in class. The way Jake felt being in that class seven hours a day, there was no way he was going to be a model student.

There was only one way to get Jake to do exactly what you wanted him to do and that was to go straight to his heart. Jake yearns for acceptance. He needs to be loved. He lives for praise. If he is denied these basic human needs he simply shuts down. He will not respond to what you want. Yell at him and you lose him. Treating him poorly, ignoring him, or humiliating him in front of others will cause him to simply draw back further within himself. Try and imagine going to a job where you received no real paycheck, the boss was constantly on you in a negative way, and your positive attributes were never recognized. How long would you give your maximum effort for this company.

Most people have the same response mechanism as my late Labrador retriever, Katy. Katy loved to have her ears rubbed. If you praised Katy, she would do about anything you wanted. In my own mind, I like to believe that she understood the words I was saying. What she really understood was how I was saying them. She understood my pleasure with her and the love I had for her based on my body language and my tone of voice. She understood my displeasure the same way. Since she basically lived for my approval, she would do whatever it took to make sure I approved of her— even when she was very sick and near death. She would work hard to do what she needed to do to gain my favor.

On her last day on this earth, I took Katy to the veterinarian because she was not responding at all to the treatment he had given her. Katy walked by my side as we entered the office. She did NOT like to go to the veterinarian, but she did because her main source of praise wanted her to go. There was another dog in the waiting room. It was about the size of a good snack for my dog. I warned her about the other dog and she seemed to understand. I told Katy to sit. She did. I rubbed her ears and neck and told her how good she was. The veterinarian picked her up and carried her into the examination room and set her on the table. She was afraid but calmed down when she felt my familiar touch on her back and face. Then ... she simply died right there while I was comforting her with my words and a gentle touch. Her last breath was on me. She responded to love right to the end.

As a middle school principal I encourage my teachers to make the word love a verb in their interaction with kids. Many of our kids come from environments where love is not practiced in the home. There may be a parent or two in the home, but the children are literally almost orphaned by the lack of care and love. There is a disease called Erasmus that babies contract in orphanages. It is fatal. The way children contract the disease is from the lack of love. Literally, I mean the lack of physical, caring contact that goes beyond simply feeding and changing of clothes. The babies become hopeless and die. What a terrible thing it would be for students at our school to live in an Erasmus state of mind. I pray it never happens.

Jake and the rest of my children, all sons, are being trained, not only by my wife and me, but by the many teachers with whom they will spend countless hours for the rest of their academic career. I am hoping that most of their teachers will care whether they learn or not. I can tell them right now that they will respond to love, caring, and understanding.

Love in the classroom is not some mushy feeling – it is a verb. It is demonstrated, as it was to my former pet, by appropriate touching, positive words, constructive feedback, and positive tones of voice. *My three (now four) sons' academic futures are largely in the hands of the teachers who will mold their dreams and develop their "bag of tools" to give them a world of opportunity.*

Whether my sons respond to their teachers is largely up to each teacher and his or her ability to see the need to "scratch my son behind the ears." In addition to being extremely tender-hearted, Jake is amazingly loyal and would run through a brick wall for anyone who treats him well and praises him when he does what the source of praise wants him to do. He just glows and works at a whole new level.

As a principal (now a superintendent), I try to model the behavior I want to see. As a Daddy it is my "number two job" (right after doing the same for my wife). My sons' futures depend upon it. Teacher, you want to know about Jake? Please, teacher, "scratch my son behind his ears." He'll be devoted to you for life.

Jake Woolf...scratch him behind the ears. ☺

Loving kids through acts and words of affirmation are huge. The first time I let folks read this essay was in the district that had Jake's teacher in it. In hindsight, I probably shouldn't have released it, but I did. I was seeing a problem with a lack of relationship between students and teachers in our school district at the time. Some teachers were amazing at it, but a large number were not. If some were offended because I called them out on it, so be it, but I wish I had found a way to soften the blow. The truth is that there is a huge difference between teaching kids and teaching curriculum. Connected, caring teachers teach kids.

To make matters worse, I have witnessed many educators behaving in ways that are destructive to building relationship. If you ask many kids if they like school, their response is usually in the negative. Some who are "teacher pleasers" or have very positive social experiences at school like it, but the usual response I get when I ask a kid if he or she likes going to school is "No." When did they decide that they didn't like going to school? After the first week or two of school when I watch our pre-school kids or our kindergarteners all I see is joy. They almost always love it! What happens to change that?

I know when each of my kids quit liking school. My oldest son was in 5th grade. We had just moved back to Kansas from Colorado. He had a 4th grade teacher, Mr. Krablean, who was amazing! He had a relationship with my son that made him love school. He even let my son babysit his garter snake over Christmas break (thanks Mr. Krablean … I'll find a way to get even some day. ☺).

We moved back to Kansas and my son, Stephen, had a brand new school to fit into. Stephen was not outgoing and the teachers didn't facilitate relationships with his peers at school. His 5th grade teacher most certainly did not have a relationship with Stephen. He was alone. Thank God we have very strong relationships in our family, or he may have been done. He used to walk along the edge of the playground every recess. No one would talk to him or walk with him. He told me he tried to play with the kids a couple of times, but they told him to go away. The teachers weren't really watching the kids … they were having their conversations and not ever really paying attention. Every day he would walk the edge of the playground alone. He was never invited to parties or over to anyone's house to play. Thankfully he had a family to play with. I used to drive by the playground during their recess from time to time and see him alone walking. It always made me cry.

On the other hand, my son, Tanner, had an amazing experience at school, and looking back, it was a result of every teacher he had making him feel valued and daring to have a relationship with him. As a result, he is considering being a teacher as well.

When did I decide I "hated" school—fourth grade. Like the rest of the kids in my class that year, I showed up with my favorite new school clothes: Sears Toughskin jeans, Keds tennis shoes, and my new Lenny Dawson #16 Kansas City Chiefs jersey. I took my position in the desk with my name on it and waited for our teacher, Mrs. … let's call her "Mrs. Crab," to step forth and impart her wisdom upon us. She had obviously been to some workshop that summer because she opened up with "This year we will be doing math at your own pace …"

Yes! My own pace was a whole different animal. 2 + 2 = 4 and after recess and perhaps a little lunch, I'll write that down! I loved this … for a while. It soon became obvious that this teaching method was not working for me. At the end of the year while everyone else was done with their math book and were working on something else, I was less than half way done with my math textbook.

Kids know whether teachers like them or not, don't they? My learning style was not working into her teaching style. I could feel her wrath as she looked at me or in the way she answered questions I had. I always felt "dumb" after she "helped" me.

Christmas break came and went and I was back to school under a new edict from Mrs. Crab. It was becoming increasingly obvious to her that I was not going to respond the way she wanted me to respond to her new teaching method. She had me come to her desk and she informed me that I would be receiving no recess until I was caught up in math. Evidently she thought that taking this semi-hyper ten-year-old and making him sit in a desk all day was a good idea.

Using deprivation did not have the impact she hoped it would. I would sit at my desk each recess while she was taking a break in the teachers' lounge and practice burping. Yes ... burping. I could get through the alphabet. I'm proud to say a couple of my sons have inherited this skill. I wonder to this day if there weren't a couple of teachers hanging out outside the classroom door timing my burps and betting on their duration. This did not make my teacher a happy camper, and I didn't care.

Since deprivation wasn't working, she resorted to another tool in her bag of tricks ... humiliation. With about three weeks left in the school year she would call me to the board in front of all of the other students in the class and give me a problem to do like multiply a three digit number times a three digit number. I had NO idea how to do this function. Instead, on a daily basis, I had the privilege of standing in front of my class and crying.

The humiliation of not knowing how to do the problem every day and the humiliation of standing there and crying in front of my classmates on a daily basis was just about more than I could bear. Getting up and going to school daily was becoming excruciating and my hate for school was beyond what my teacher, Mrs. Crab, could possibly imagine. As I write about it now or any time I talk about it, the pain and shame come rushing back and it is a rarity that tears don't come to my eyes.

The school year ended, and they moved me to fifth grade. They probably shouldn't have, but they did. I was NOT looking forward to the school year. My summer of never ending baseball, TV cartoons, vacation with my family, fishing, camping out, and running with my friends was now over and the school year was now at hand.

The new 5th grade teacher, Miss Haslouer, walked into the room. She was a brand new teacher that had come to us from what I like to call "the Harvard of the Midwest"—Kansas State University. When she walked into the room, she did so in a manner that instantly made it obvious that she had some pretty severe disabilities in her legs and then we noticed the same with her arms. I'm ashamed to say that my first thought was, "Oh, great … I had "Mrs. Crab" last year and now look what I've got." That thought was to change soon.

She did three things that changed my life that year. The first thing she did was to tell us that she loved us. The second thing she did was to love us. As was stated in the "essay" I wrote to my teachers earlier in this chapter, love is a verb! We knew she loved us by the way she took time to connect with us. She knew what we liked and didn't like, and she let us get to know her as well. We knew why she walked the way she did and why her arms worked the way they did—polio. She shared deeply about her life, and we shared deeply with her or as deeply as fifth grade students get. She was amazing.

The third thing she did involved a cardboard box that once carried Clorox bottles. She filled it with rubber spiders, rubber snakes, rubber monsters, Krackle bars, 3 Musketeer bars, Snicker bars, and Baby Ruth bars. If you performed well enough, you had the opportunity to leave your desk, be publically recognized by walking across the classroom, and choosing a prize out of the cardboard box. It wasn't so much the prize as it was the recognition of a job well done. We wanted to make her proud, and we wanted the rest of the class to know that we are doing well, me especially after the year before.

I caught up in math and passed most of the other students in the class. I got through calculus in high school. I would have been dead in the water academically if it weren't for Miss Haslouer. She connected with us, and it changed our lives for the better. Without her, I would not have had any of the wonderful experiences I have had in my life. Academically, it would not have been possible. She put me back on the right track with the right attitude to go forth and be whatever I wanted to be.

I believe that we as educators need to model what we want to see in our students. One of the things I want to see in our students is gratitude toward their teachers and the ability to express gratitude toward those who impact their lives. I finally got around to this the first few years that I was a principal.

Miss Haslouer had left the little town of Claflin, Kansas after a few years and moved to Wichita, Kansas where she had the audacity to get married. She was now Mrs. Bevilacqua. She had children of her own and had adopted babies, some with severe mental and physical disabilities. At least one she loved literally until death. Although not teaching, she was continuing her heroic life as a mother. As luck would have it, I found out where she lived.

I was in Wichita for a state-wide conference for administrators and I took it upon myself to skip a session to go see Miss Haslouer, now Mrs. Bevilacqua, to let her know how important she was in my life and to thank her for loving us and changing our lives for the better. I knocked on the door, and she answered with one of the babies in her arms. I exclaimed, "It's me! Steve Woolf from your first fifth grade class in Claflin!"

She invited me right in. I kind of knew that she really had no idea who I was, but she recognized the name. I could have been the BTK

Killer, but she invited me right on in. I explained who I was, and then I thanked her for the life changing impact she had on me and to let her know that I knew I would be nothing without her. She was in tears and so was I.

Later that year I was speaking at a graduation in Wichita at Century II Coliseum. I was talking about her and I said, "I don't know … you might even be here. Are you here?!?"

That is when I saw a hand go up in the balcony of the Coliseum. There she was … my teacher. I could barely hold it together. There she was, and she's still there for me even now. I am a blessed man.

In 2003 I was fortunate enough to be able to tell a large audience about Miss Haslouer/Mrs. Bevilacqua at the ending session at a National Renaissance Conference (a national education conference that focuses on building amazing school culture) put on by Jostens. When I finished my story, there wasn't a dry eye in the place, and then they walked her out on stage. My teacher!!! I received the gift of being able to acknowledge and love her in front of all of those people. Tears flowed throughout the auditorium. Jostens had brought her down to Dallas, Texas from Wichita, Kansas and treated her like a queen. She was there to be honored, and she had earned it.

My teacher: God bless you. Thank you for "Scratching me behind my ears."

Miss Haslouer (Mrs. Louise Bevilacqua)

Check out the Chapter 5 "Post Chapter Video" on You Tube at the following:

https://www.youtube.com/watch?v=-tDPSmC2xRo

Chapter 6 - Shame: The Mortal Enemy of Connection

"Shame is a soul eating emotion." – Carl Jung (founder of Analytical Psychology)

"The revolt against one's environment is usually 'shame' of one's environment." – Czeslaw Milosz (Nobel Prize Winning Author)

"Shame is the intensely painful feeling or experience of believing we are flawed and therefore unworthy of acceptance and belonging." - Brene' Brown (author/sociologist)

Over the past quarter of a century as an educator and a half a century of life, I have experienced and seen the damage that shame can inflict on the lives of students and the rest of society. Looking at Brene' Brown's definition of shame that grew out of her work on shame, connection, and vulnerability, most of us are having flashbacks to very, very personal tapes that run inside our head of experiences that have left us feeling unconnected—unworthy of acceptance and belonging.

Man innately strives for connection. It is a constant drive, and it gives purpose and meaning to life. Shame is a poison that can debilitate a life.

I have had a couple of experiences in the past few years that have brought the debilitating power of shame to light. One personal experience I had was going through *Break Through* training under the direction of Dr. Paul Fitzgerald.[5] Dr. Paul deals directly with shame and helping participants see the real self vs. the self who has tapes of shame running rampant, rendering the ability to experience joy and connection obsolete.

While the experience of going through several long days of *Break Through* workshops was powerful, nothing brought the power of shame vs. the power of connection more to light for me than the story of a child I met when he moved into a small school district in central Kansas.

The student was a 13-year-old African American boy who moved into the school district for the second half of the school year. January in Kansas was an inhospitable place where a bitterly cold wind cut through his inadequate jacket the foster home had given him as he walked up the sidewalk of the small, Pre-K through 8th grade school building. The central Kansas school rarely had students who weren't white. He was the only African American child. He came in the middle of the year because he was relocated into a foster home that had a reputation for being notoriously bad. He had been in SRS custody since the age of

5   BreakThrough,   Heart   Connexion   Seminars, http://www.heartconnexion.org/index.html

three when he was found on the streets of Wichita, KS, naked, cut up, and drunk in freezing temperatures. To this day, he says that he can still remember how badly his feet hurt as a result of the cold.

All parental rights were severed from the heavily chemically dependent mother, who was extremely abusive in addition to this incident. Rights were severed from a chemically dependent, incarcerated biological father who had no attachment to the boy's biological mother other than to father this child. This child was bounced around the state to many terrible foster homes where he experienced every type of abuse you can imagine. His life was a living hell.

Being a foster child, he got the least of everything. Name brand clothing or shoes were not going to happen for him. Fancy electronic devices and other popular toys most of his classmates had were just a dream. Someone to truly love him was just another pipe dream.

This boy was initially placed in special education because he couldn't read. This was cured in the fifth grade when one of the foster homes locked him in his room every day when he came home from school. There he had nothing in the room but his bed, his clothes, and one book. That book was about Greek mythology and all of the related stories.

With no interaction with anyone or anything

else, this book totally accepted him without judgment and he spent all of his time with it. He eventually taught himself to read using this book and became what most of us would probably consider an expert in Greek mythology. Many have made the "mistake" with this young man of bringing up a subject that pertains to Greek mythology and immediately set themselves up for a lengthy lecture on the subject. He rarely pronounced any of the names correctly because he had never heard them; he just read them.

He was moved out of that foster home to horrendous foster homes in southeastern Kansas where he lived out unspeakable abuse at the hands of other foster brothers and sisters in the same homes. The family that locked him in a room, a very religious family, decided that God had told them to adopt the young man. He was moved back to them and they did, in fact, adopt him.

The mental abuse did not lessen. They put an alarm on his bedroom door and let him know that if he were to step out of the door in the night, he would be severely punished. Like most of us, he had to use the restroom at some point during the night but feared the retribution of the adoptive parents if he were to step out of the room. Being a resourceful young man after years of being forced to be resourceful, he found a way to relieve himself where no one would know and he would be able to avoid the punishment of stepping out of his room to use the restroom. There was a heating/AC register on the floor of his room … enough said. Naturally, as time went on, the smell became intense, and the adoptive parents found out.

This, among other small incidents that frustrated the adoptive parents, was an impetus to cause more shame in the life of this young man. The adoptive parents sat him down and told him that they were going to "un-adopt" him. They were sending him back into the system. To do this, they had to have at least two meetings with the SRS where they sat down with the adopted child, looked him in the eyes, and told him that they do not want him as their son any more. They were required to do this not once, but at least twice. The feelings of pain and shame that were building up inside of him were nearly debilitating. Every connection thus far in his life had been shattered.

That is when he was shipped to the small school district in central Kansas and put into a non-caring, non-loving, terrible environment in a new foster home with many other foster children who attended the school district as well. He would show up at school every day with a pocket size New Testament Bible tucked in his back pocket and read it at recess in hopes that his old adoptive home would hear about it and want to take him back. He also worked extremely hard to get straight "A's" for the same reason. He was hoping that they would find him worthy of love, acceptance, and grace. That didn't happen.

The summer before his eighth grade year his school had a big "welcome back to school" swimming party for the students before the school year started. One of his foster parents showed up at the school parking lot with a pickup full of kids—none buckled in because there were more kids than buckles—and dumped them off. The students got on the bus and proceeded to the pool at a nearby community in the district. The young man was the only African American child in the school, so he did stand out. He also stood out because he was extremely polite and enjoyed the swimming party immensely.

When the party ended, the students were loaded on the bus and were taken back to the school. The school district was very spread out, and the principal of that school, who was driving the bus, needed to take kids to two other drop-off points to be picked up by their parents. His wife supervised the kids where this young man was dropped off while her husband delivered kids to their destinations.

The time for picking up the kids had come and gone. It ended up being just this child and the principal's wife visiting for another hour until the foster parents picked him up. It was obvious to all by the demeanor of the foster parents that this young man was not loved, wanted, or appreciated. His whole being cried out for connection, but all he was left with was a sense of worthlessness and shame.

The young man was very athletic and wanted to play football, but the foster parents wouldn't get him a physical, football shoes, or a ride into town from the foster home six miles out in the country for the two weeks of summer football practice. Finally, after the season had already started, they allowed him to play because there was an athletic bus that would take him home. The school provided the shoes from a collection of used shoes left behind by former student athletes over the years. Were the foster parents ever at any event or game in which this young man participated? You know the answer.

Basketball started in late October of that year. One thing led to another and the principal of the young man's school ended up being the boys' basketball coach that year. This young man was allowed to play because there was an athletic bus to deliver him to the foster home after practice. He worked extremely hard on the court and off. He had earned a 4.0 GPA the nine-week grade period before this and showed the same type of effort on the basketball court. The school colors were blue and white, but he was stuck with a pair of off-brand, thrift store, red and white basketball shoes. They were size 12 on his size 13 feet. When the PE teacher purchased him a pair of Adidas basketball shoes that fit for Christmas that year, the foster parents were extremely upset and told the principal to make sure that no one in the school would do that for this kid again. This foster "mom" had no desire to help this kid through the shame that he felt. In fact, she acted on the belief that if she kept him down, kept him feeling shame, he was much easier to handle.

Through conversations with this young man, the principal had learned that this student had never been out of the state of Kansas. The principal's family was going to Colorado the day after Christmas to visit friends and relatives. The principal and his wife thought it would be good for this boy to accompany them on this trip and see the Rocky Mountains for the first time. The foster parents readily agreed to this because that meant they would be rid of him for a week and still get paid.

The principal and his family had to remember that any social grace that the student knew, he had picked up himself. This meant that he was going to make a lot of mistakes socially. Any interaction he had with another human was filtered through his life experience of mistrust, abuse, and shame. In order to protect himself, he had to assume any adult he associated with was going to hurt him at some point.

The principal had three sons, and they were with them on the Colorado trip. The student was much more enamored with the principal's sons' electronic games than he was with the grandeur of the Rocky Mountains. He was trying to experience all the activities he knew would be impossible to do upon his return. The principal's sons introduced him to sledding in Colorado and he took to it with reckless abandon. He showed absolutely no concern for himself or his own well being while sledding. The principal's wife made him wear a motorcycle helmet because she was sure he was going to hurt himself badly.

They stayed much of the time in Colorado at the home of the principal's father-in-law. He was a very generous man and one evening handed out $100 bills to each of his children and grandchildren who were there. He asked the principal if he minded if he gave a $100 bill to the student as well. The principal knew that the student had probably never seen $100 before, let alone have $100 of his own, so he happily agreed to let the generosity of his father-in-law be bestowed on this student. The reaction that the principal's father-in-law received from this young man was of a value much greater than the $100 bill that exchanged hands. The student started to dream of all that he could purchase and the people he could help with such a huge treasure.

The principal would later share that the young man was a picture of Ruby Payne's study of the spending habits of people in poverty.[6] The young man knew that he had to spend the money before he got back to his foster parent's house because they would take the money from him, and he would never see it again. The young man spent all but $20 on items with Nike emblems on them. The foster parents took the twenty dollars that remained. He would not see it again.

Now and then the young man would trust the principal and his wife with a story of his past. They tried hard not to act shocked, but they would tell you that they weren't sure how good they were at this. When they arrived back in Kansas, the student let them know that this trip had been the greatest time in his life. Then he headed back to his life in "the system."

The principal could feel the sadness, shame, and total lack of worth by which this young man was absolutely inundated. The lack of connection this young man was dealing with was debilitating. The student continued to see himself as unworthy of love and connection due to a life of rejection and horrific experiences of abuse.

The end of the basketball season was approaching, and his foster parents had not been to one game. They would dump the other foster kids off at the game but never bother to step in the gym in support. The young man really wanted his foster mother to see him play. He could not care

[6] Payne, Ruby. *"A Framework For Understanding Poverty."* Baytown, TX. RFT, 1995.

less whether the foster father would see him play because of the constant cut-downs and emotional abuse that he put him through. The foster mother did the same, but at least she fed the kids most of the time.

Finally, the last game of the year came, and the young man was so excited because his foster mother promised she would come and see him play! He couldn't stop talking about it with the coach/principal. The foster mother had told him that she was going to bring a camera and film him playing. The principal had a gut feeling that this was not going to end well.

Game time came. No foster Mom. The foster boy was sure she was just late. The principal called his wife to come and cheer the student on because he believed the foster mom would not be there. The game came and went and no foster mom. The student was extremely depressed after the game. The next day the principal asked what had happened. The student said that the foster mother told him that she had heard from one of the other foster kids that he had called her a name. She told him that she was never coming to any event of his from then on. He insisted that he did not call her a name, but the foster mother would not believe him. Either way, she let him down. Again.

Brene' Brown's research on shame found that people fell into two groups—people who have a sense of love and belonging and those who do not.

Her findings seem simplistic, yet the research is clear. The difference between the two groups is that those who have a sense of love and belonging believe they are worthy of love and belonging. That's it; they believe they are worthy of connection. Those who do not have a sense of love and belonging and believe they are not worthy of love are debilitated by shame.

This student definitely fell into the second category. The ability to trust others and feel that he was worthy of connection had been continually battered. Shame is a fear of disconnection. The student feared that people would know of the horrid abuse of all types that he had experienced his whole life. The fact that some of it was sexual in nature made it even worse for this student in his own mind. His constant worry was that people would find out about these experiences that debilitated him.

What the student really needed to know is that everybody feels shame of some sort. The only people who do not feel shame are sociopaths who have no capacity for human empathy or connection. The student feared that if people knew him deeply they would find him unworthy of connection, and that held him hostage. In fact, he had already decided that he was unworthy, even though he continued to try to find a way out of the bondage of shame and the lack of connection it brings.

As educators, we must realize that to truly make a difference in the lives of our students, we must move beyond the written curriculum and the pedagogy of teaching methods and classroom management. We have to be leaders in making connections with students. To do this we must be willing to make ourselves vulnerable, make ourselves truly "seen" by our students. Brene' Brown describes this as "deeply seen."

Overcoming shame requires work. It requires persistence, and it requires an "I will love you no matter what" attitude from everyone who helps those holding onto shame. It requires a breakthrough.

Check out the Chapter 6 "Post Chapter Video" on You Tube at the following:

https://www.youtube.com/watch?v=WVJD pDXyht8

Chapter 7 - Breaking Through Shame

"What do you regard as most humane? To spare someone shame." - Friedrich Nietzsche

"Shame should be reserved for things we choose to do, not the circumstances that life puts us in."
- Ann Patchett, "Truth and Beauty"

Gravity is a powerful force. The physical laws of nature are very difficult to battle against. I don't know if anyone has experienced a feeling that I clearly felt while out on a very high bridge in Colorado. The Royal Gorge Bridge is a suspension bridge that hangs 955 feet above the Arkansas River that roars through the canyon below. The Royal Gorge was the highest bridge until recently when a bridge in China surpassed it. Being a flatlander from Kansas, stepping out on the bridge was always an adventure. Every time I eased myself over to the rail and looked over the edge to the flowing river far below, I felt this pull—almost an urge to go over the rail. I know this sounds weird, but I now know the pull was gravity.

As I get older, and unfortunately gain more "mass," I am feeling the impact of gravity more and more. Jumping up out of bed or off the ground was never a problem. I am feeling it now. In addition to being impacted by a physical law that states that everything goes from a state or order to disorder, gravity is keeping the man down! Gravity is providing a constant struggle.

Shame has the power of gravity in the lives of those who experience it. It has a downward pull that debilitates those who allow it to build up. Overcoming the powerful debilitating force of shame takes very hard work. It doesn't happen by accident. It takes work, and it takes help.

It seems that much of our society has tried to medicate their way out of the terrible impact shame has on their life. While I truly believe that there are chemical imbalances that impact some people that cause severe depression and that those people can be helped through the use of medication, I also believe that there are those who choose to dull the pain of shame through the same types of medication, legal or not.

One of the many problems with medicating shame is that much more than shame is dulled. Joy, happiness, pain, ache, anger or any type of feeling, physical or mental, is dulled as well. Life is dulled. Life is messy, happy, sad, and joyful. Dulling one of these through medication dulls them all. Whether it is an actual prescription, a prescription drug taken without a prescription, alcohol, or illegal drugs, all are ways to medicate shame that are ultimately ineffective and leave the "medicated" person with the same shame only usually at a higher level.

When I think of the boy in the foster care

system from the previous chapter who continually lived in a situation where he was torn down, abused, and made to feel shame on a daily basis, the courage that it took to get up every morning and keep going starts to become mind boggling.

It reminds me of a wonderful Winston Churchill quote where he said, "Courage is rightly esteemed the first of human qualities ... because it is the quality that guarantees all others." The young man had courage. Were there fears? I'm sure there were many. In order to be brave, one must first have fear to overcome. Fear begets courage, which begets bravery. This kid had it in spades.

In today's society, we find people medicating themselves chemically with drugs such as meth that makes the "medicated" feel invincible with chemical courage. We see the same with alcohol and other drugs as well. To be able to get up every morning, look life in the eye, and attack it head on is special. It is the type of behavior we want in all of our kids and adults for that matter.

Unfortunately, life's battles can be fought with great courage, but shame can still have a tight grip. Gravity still works. To overcome the debilitating grip of shame takes people ... special people.

People who will fight "gravity" in helping others through shame are special. The battle is hard and it takes work, dedication, love, understanding, and patience. Ultimately, it will take a breakthrough for the person who is shame filled and the "gravity busters" are key to the process. It is also key that the "gravity buster" had experienced a breakthrough from the power of shame as well.

The foster boy that I have shared with you experienced this breakthrough in his life. The principal and his wife made the decision that if they invested four years of their lives in this foster child, gave him a home, gave him a name, and gave him unconditional love, he could make it. With that thought in mind, they brought him into their home and adopted him. While that may seem like the happy ending, it is really just the beginning of the healing for this child who was just 14 at the time.

The surface level was easy. All of this child's clothing and shoes had been second hand or Wal-Mart specials. When the hateful foster father dropped the boy off at his new adoptive home, he had some of his clothing in trash bags. The foster family kept the BB gun he had received for Christmas from a volunteer that put together Christmas presents for kids in need, along with a cheap little MP3 player, and all of his coats. They called it "community property." The adoptive family told him not to worry; they had him covered.

Over the next few weeks, the former foster boy and now adoptive son of the principal and his wife was clothed with new quality clothing. They replaced the property that had been stolen from him by the foster family. He had all of the clothing and "things" that other kids in his school with families had. He had a name. He was the son of the principal, which had definite advantages and disadvantages. He had great food as well. He was involved in positive social activities and athletics. He now had an extended family beyond his new siblings that made a concerted effort to love him.

All of this was wonderful for this young man who had lived a very, very rough life to that point, but it was not the breakthrough that the young man needed. This young man had endured many horrible experiences of all nature at the hands of women that were put into his life. If you let your imagination go here, you will probably be pretty accurate on his life experience. The abuse started as a baby and carried on through his most recent foster mother. As a result of this abuse, the young man held deep resentment and a great lack of respect for women. This was a product of the shame he felt having gone through these experiences. He was tough, but he was hurt and damaged.

As with most relationships, this new family relationship started sweet and clean. No one revealed any deep feelings because they did not know each other well yet. Depth takes time and trust. The first step of commitment had been taken, but this young man had a family commit to him before and then throw him back in the "system."

Anger and disrespect started to surface as a result of the shame he carried. There were some extreme acts of disrespect and the disregard of boundaries that resulted in a very serious situation in the new family. In a foster care situation, the young man would be moved to a new family immediately. He fully expected this. He was sure that all of the amazing things that had been happening for him were now over, and he would be going back into the system.

The shame he felt because of the fact that the newly adopted father knew of the disrespect he had shown to his foster mother was huge. He was set up for either a breakdown or a breakthrough. The interesting thing is that making or breaking this young man was entirely in the hands of the "gravity buster" principal/dad. He could have let him dwell in the land of shame and turn him back into the system, or he could facilitate a breakthrough.

The adoptive parents decided on grace, acceptance, and unconditional love. These are great tools to work through shame. The young man had rarely cried in his life. Tears now came down in a torrent because he feared all was lost. The principal told him that there was nothing he could do that would make him love him less or let him go. These are words that the young man had never heard.

They talked about the incidents that happened with their family, and the horrid incidents of the past for this young man came roaring back. It was the first time he had ever talked about it. The young man shared that he was sure he could never go to heaven because the things he was forced to do were so bad. The principal/dad spent the next couple hours talking about grace, forgiveness, and love—amazing tools to overcome shame. The young man showed powerful courage to face his demons and the shame that controlled his life. He asked for help. He got it and more.

The next months and years were full of grace-filled, open, honest, loving conversations. The young man hated counselors because none of them addressed the source of the pain, and many wanted to just medicate him. He now trusted his new parents enough to allow them to schedule time with a counselor who specialized in shame and breakthrough. They met individually and as a family. The young man broke through the hold of shame and was able to continue to stay out of its hold when it crept back by coming to an understanding of forgiveness, grace, and love.

He now understood that he was absolutely deserving of love and he did NOT deserve shame. He trusted the "gravity breakers" in his life and he is a young man who has every opportunity to be a wonderful husband, dad, and friend as he continues to fight the gravity of shame. He has connection, and he has love. He also has a Dad … me.

Kellie, Chris, and Steve Woolf – Senior Night

Check out the Chapter 7 Post-Chapter Video on You Tube at the following:

http://youtu.be/0poQ-vUpRIs

Chapter 8 - The Medicine of Vulnerability

"We share with those who have earned the right to hear the story." - Brene' Brown

"No significant learning happens without significant relationship." - Dr. James Comer

"Love is the ultimate and the highest goal to which a man can aspire." - Dr. Viktor Frankl

One of my favorite people ever was Mr. Rogers! Fred Rogers displayed a real persona on PBS that made everyone believe that this is a man I could trust and would care for me. We felt we knew him. Mr. Rogers kept a quote in his wallet from an unknown social worker that said, "Frankly, there isn't anybody you couldn't learn to love once you've heard their story." This is beautiful, true, and very difficult to get to the point where you get to hear another's story.

If you happen to go to church and you are an educator, then you have probably been approached to teach a Sunday school class. The pressure is on at that point because now you have to be amazing because that is your profession. It is a little like being a professional comedian and someone catching you on the street and have them ask you to "say something funny" … the pressure is on!

I was asked recently to teach a Sunday school class, and I thought I knew exactly how to design the class. Understanding the power of "story" and the way Jesus taught in parables, I thought it would be fun to study the parables and then take it a step further. I would have those who attended the class tell their story. They could share the story of their life, and we would all draw closer together by getting real with one another and sharing deeply about ourselves.

I shared this idea with my wife, and she looked at me like I had lost my mind! She said that she wouldn't even go to my Sunday school class if that was what she was going to have to do. I couldn't believe it … my own wife! Then it hit me like a brick. Just because I was willing to make myself vulnerable to the class did not mean they had any desire at all to share their story with me. I had not earned the right to hear everyone's story. Lesson learned.

For years I wondered what it was that made kids open up with their life's experience to some teachers while other teachers never had a student open up to them beyond the curriculum at hand. Why do some teachers never have an appropriate relationship with students that moves beyond just the curriculum when the research shows us so clearly the positive impact on learning that relationships produce?

Dr. James Comer stated, "No significant

learning happens without significant relationship."[7] Since we know that we all innately strive for connection, it seemed that being able to break through the barriers with kids ought to be a no brainer, but it simply was not happening. There are very few times I know of students actually opening up to teachers. There may very well be real problems that were significant barriers to the student performing well in school, but it seems that most students simply will not share. What I discovered is that most teachers have not earned the right to hear the student's story. The truth is that a huge number of teachers I have worked with in my quarter century+ in schools have not really gotten real with themselves—let alone students. Brene' Brown says that if you don't know how to do vulnerability, then vulnerability is doing you. Vulnerability is the door to connection.[8]

I had a student bring this home to me in a very clear way. I will call the student "Bobby" and not use his real name. If you've ever watched the cartoon series "King of the Hill" then you would know exactly what Bobby looked like because he very closely resembled Bobby Hill from this cartoon complete with the buzz haircut because he was constantly fighting lice.

---

[7] Comer, James, "Leave No Child Behind: Preparing Today's Youth For Tomorrow's World," Yale University Press: New Haven and London, 2005.

[8] Brown, Brene', "Oprah's Lifeclass: Part 1," OWN, 2013.

Since Bobby struggled greatly in the classroom and was a frequent flier to the office for discipline reasons, I ended up visiting often with Bobby's parents. Because their phone was rarely connected, I ended up going to Bobby's house regularly. Bobby's parents suffered from severe alcoholism, and when they were drunk enough, they would actually let me in the house.

What I observed was sickening. Left over pizza was ground into the carpet along with other substances that I couldn't identify, yet I could smell. I saw roaches run along the walls. I could see back into the kitchen, and the sink was full of dirty pots and pans with the exception of one that was on the floor with a dog working to empty the contents. There was visual and aromatic evidence that there were cats and probably no litter box. Cigarette smoke filled the air and there were piles of dirty clothing. The curtains had feces on them. This is where Bobby lived.

You can imagine how hard it was to come to school clean living in this environment. So we had Bobby who showed up to school everyday looking like Bobby Hill, smelling like the inside of his house, and reaping the results of a home where there was zero support for learning. You can imagine how eighth grade students treated Bobby. You can also imagine the shame that Bobby carried around with him daily.

In our school, we worked hard to celebrate

our teachers as well as our students. One way we did this was by having a "Staff Member of the Month" award. Instead of selecting one staff member that was "best" for that month, we handled it differently. Even though teachers are like most people and like to be complimented, they are very uncomfortable when one of them is selected as being "best." Teachers are used to being treated the same. They all get paid basically the same (with a little survival pay for hanging in there year after year) no matter how hard or little they work. When one is lifted up over the others, often times it is uncomfortable.

To avoid this we had students, fellow educators, or parents nominate staff members for something special they observed them doing or knew about them doing. We would receive up to 150 nominations per month. We would draw one out of the box where the nominations were turned in and call that person the "Staff Member of the Month."

We would put together a bulletin board about the staff member and load them up with prizes. The remaining nomination forms that stated why they were nominated were put into the staff members' boxes, and it became like Valentine's Day!

Staff members that never checked their mailboxes rushed down to see if they received nominations with compliments written on them.

Some teachers received a box stuffed full of them. Some teachers received none, and there was a reason. They had not developed positive relationships with kids.

Bobby had nominated a staff member the kids called "Hud." Larry Hudson was a superb industrial arts teacher who looked like he belonged in a biker gang. The reason I remember this is because Bobby wrote the most powerful thing I have ever seen written about a teacher. It is so powerful that I committed it to memory. This came from a young man steeped in poverty and shame.

Bobby had filled out the nomination form...

Name: Bobby V.

Nominee: Hud

Date: 14 (?)

And then he wrote the most powerful statement I have ever seen written about an educator. It read ... **Reason educator nominated:** *He treats me rite* (sp).

When this was drawn out of the box and I saw it for the first time, I had to excuse myself, go to my office, and let the tears flow. Knowing the burden of pain and shame that Bobby carried on a daily basis and how kids treated him ... how some educators treated him made this statement about Hud even more powerful!

Larry Hudson had dared to love this kid. Knowing Hud, he probably wouldn't call it love, but I know it when I see it. He would talk to Bobby, treat him with respect, not avoid him, and make him feel like he was as important as anybody else in the class. No one else was able to do this for Bobby. Hud had earned the right to hear Bobby's story. Mr. Hudson had made himself vulnerable to the possibility of Bobby rejecting him as was Bobby's habit.

Bobby had been hurt so often that he knew if he rejected you first, then he wouldn't have to worry about being rejected by you. I have no doubt that Bobby did reject Hud at first, but Larry did not take it personally. He kept at it. He opened up to Bobby about his hobbies, riding his Harley, and hunting. He teased Bobby without cutting him down and allowed Bobby to return the favor. He got real with Bobby. He reached Bobby. He treated Bobby "rite (sp)."

The trouble is that sometimes we like students so much more than the students like themselves. The student finds it hard to believe that you will find value in them. We carry the "medicine" of relationship as a result of vulnerability. Many educators who are good at this find themselves with a common problem. They only have so much "medicine" to dispense, and they forget to replenish.

A man who gave a great demonstration of this while going through the horrific experience of being detained in Nazi concentration camps was Viktor Frankl. Dr. Frankl, a neuroscientist and psychologist, wrote the groundbreaking book "Man's Search For Meaning." I recently read this book again and ran into morsels of wisdom like "Love is the ultimate and the highest goal to which a man can aspire" and one of my favorite quotes "Love is the only way to grasp another human being in the innermost core of his personality. No one can become fully aware of the very essence of another human being unless he loves him."[9]

As an educator, making yourself vulnerable to relationship and pouring yourself or your "medicine" into a relationship for the betterment of our students is hard work. It is easy to get burnt out. Viktor Frankl had a similar experience in the concentration camps.

I was involved in a workshop that focused on working on "me" with Dr. Paul Fitzgerald a few years ago, and he told us a story to start an exercise. I have used this exercise many times since while working with educators. It was a story about Viktor Frankl.

The time Viktor spent in the concentration camps was life changing to say the least. A trained psychologist with medical training as well, Viktor spent the majority of his time in captivity building roads for the Nazis. At one point later in his time of captivity, he was put in the position where he was to care for others in the concentration camp who

_____

[9] Frankl, Viktor, "Man's Search For Meaning," Beacon Press: Boston, MA, 1959.

had typhoid fever. They were dying quickly, and since no Nazi wanted to risk catching this highly communicable disease, Viktor was "volunteered" to care for these that were in peril. It made little difference to the Nazi captors whether Viktor caught typhoid fever or not. He would likely be exterminated at some point anyway.

Viktor was given very little medication and food to take care of any of their symptoms. He was given a small handful of aspirin, some very weak soup, and that was it. He realized going in that he was going to have to do triage to figure out where he should invest the possibly life saving aspirin.

Those that he found that were too far gone and would be dead soon, he comforted the best he could, but he did not invest medication. He gave them just enough soup to keep them comfortable. Since most were starving already, the lack of food was not a shock to their system.

He also withheld medicine from those that had the symptoms but seemed on the road to recovery. They received food, but no aspirin would be given to relive the pain. Viktor was looking for those that would have a chance of living if he intervened with the medicine to help control their body temperature. A mixture of aspirin and weak soup would give them a fighting chance to beat the fever and a chance to survive the concentration camp.

This would require Viktor Frankl to look each

of these men in the eye and say either, "I have medicine for you," or "I have no medicine for you." Each statement meant life or death to two-thirds of the men that he cared for.

After sharing this story with the workshop participants, who had spent many days working on ourselves and becoming somewhat close, Dr. Paul put the eighteen of us in a circle and gave us an assignment. One at a time, we were to rise out of our chair and stand in front of each person in our group and say to them either "I have medicine for you" or "I have no medicine for you." He then let us know that we could have only four doses of medicine that we could administer. Four friends would be given life saving medicine while thirteen of our friends we would not be able to give medicine to, thus condemning them to death.

There were tears as each of us took a turn giving one of two responses to each person as we stood in front of them and looked in their eyes with our verdict. When you had made your circle, you sat back down and each of the teammates stopped, looked you in the eye, and gave one of two responses. Although it was just an imaginary exercise, it still caused stress and heartache.

At the end of the exercise, Dr. Paul asked for thoughts on the exercise. People shared, some tearfully, of their struggle in deciding who they would give medicine to and who they would not.

After the group had a chance to share their

thoughts and feelings, Dr. Paul asked them a key question, "How many of you gave medication to yourself?" The answer there and with every group I have shared this with is the same. None.

Dr. Paul went on to share that when Viktor Frankl was in this situation in the concentration camp, he realized that none of them had a chance of survival if he did not remain healthy. This required him to make sure he gave himself medicine when he needed it. He needed to be very sensitive to his self so that he would know when he needed medicine. Those that he was serving— those whose lives Viktor Frankl held in his hand— counted on him to make the choice of taking care of himself first. They required him to take medicine as needed. Without it he was of no use to them.

We have to work on ourselves first in order to be able to reach others. The tough part is to get the help we need to work on ourselves. It takes bravery (because there is definitely fear involved), the willingness to be real, and the willingness to truly connect with another human being in a very real way. The trouble is finding someone who has earned the right to our vulnerability, the right to hear and know the truth about us and the struggles we have. If this is true for adults, imagine how much of a struggle it is for a child, adolescent, or young man or woman.

Check out the Chapter 8 "The Medicine of

Vulnerability" Post-Chapter Video on You Tube at the following:

http://youtu.be/PGHi55Gs2SQ

Chapter 9 - The Steepness of the Hill

"Focus on the journey, not the destination. Joy is found not in finishing an activity but in doing it."
- *Greg Anderson, Author and founder of The Wellness Project*

"No member of a crew is praised for the rugged individuality of his rowing."
- *Ralph Waldo Emerson*

I am not sure how it happened, but sometime during my second year of teaching, a veteran teacher talked me into accompanying him on a ten-day backpack trip with nine ninth grade students in the Rocky Mountains of Colorado. The class was called "Colorado Field Ecology." The further up the mountain we trekked, the more names I came up with for the class. I'm guessing that when this veteran teacher, Marc Linton, looked at me he was thinking, "He looks like he could haul a lot of gear on his back up a mountain." Yes, I'm pretty sure my Colorado Field Ecology teaching experience started as the designated pack mule.

Looking back, it was a wonderful experience and relationships were built on this journey to last a lifetime. That particular group of kids is in their late thirties now, and I am in contact with most of them, although we are spread throughout the nation. I was able to learn from a master teacher about how to conduct this type of class that immerses kids in an environment that they have not experienced before.

We hiked and backpacked in Rocky Mountain National Park, the Sand Dunes National Park, the University of Colorado Research Site, and ultimately at Rawah Wilderness Area in north central Colorado. We were heading eight and a half miles up the mountain. "Up" is the key word here. Another word I should probably inject into this story is "Steep." I would NEVER have chosen to simply grab a backpack full of gear and take off up a mountain 8.5 miles alone. The madness of the mob is what got me up the mountain. The fellowship of friends is what carried me along.

We had more fun sitting around a campfire in the evenings, sneaking rocks into one another's backpacks and under tents. We talked about life, our future, and stupid/funny stuff that ninth grade students can come up with. We fished together, and ate the fish together. Relationships were built. Connection was built. We became more and more vulnerable to one another and risked deepening friendship.

The 8.5 mile trip down the mountain was almost a celebration. We were away from base for three and a half days. One of the girls swore that she was NOT going to use "the trowel" on the trip. The yellow, or "golden" trowel was used to dig a small hole. I'll let your imagination come up with the rest. Needless to say, she was in a big hurry to get back down the mountain. About half way down, we finally told her that she might want to open her pack and take the large rock out of it because it had probably traveled far enough. If my memory serves me right, she basically sprinted the last two miles down the trail so she could answer nature's call in the outhouse at the base. She made her goal and made all of us laugh. (She is still making people laugh in her radio show out of Kansas City, not to mention any names ... Dana Wright.) We all accomplished something big together. A connection was made that could only be made through this type of experience. It was forged through physical pain and extreme challenge. I am not sure any of us, with the exception of the great teacher, Marc Linton, would have made it to the top in the time we did alone.

There is a wonderful study conducted by the University of Virginia to observe if having social support can affect the perception of the steepness of a hill. Researchers would put weights on the people in the study, and then have them indicate how steep the hill in front of them was. They discovered that participants who were accompanied by a friend estimated the hill to be less steep when compared to those who took the study alone. Even if they just thought of a supportive friend while estimating the steepness of the hill made a difference, and they judged the hill as less steep.

In both studies that were conducted, they noticed a direct correlation between the strength of the friendship, whether the friend was present or not, and how steep the hill was judged to be. Those who held a longer friendship and were closer and warmer toward one another judged the hill to be less steep. They discovered that mood, social desirability, and social facilitation did not have an impact. The study clearly demonstrated that social support is key to taking on difficult tasks such as hiking up a hill and can influence the perception of how difficult the task is.

The study called social support "interpersonal phenomenon." It could just as easily be called "connection." Whatever we choose to call it, the study shows us that friendships are beneficial when taking on difficult tasks. It also shows that the deeper the connection between the friends, the easier the perception is of the task.[10]

How many of our kids are going it alone? We know the research. We know that alone, the hill looks steeper. Many of us have made the decision in life when looking at a challenge that was especially daunting to simply not do it.

Connection seems to build bravery in the face of fear that increases exponentially as the strength

---

[10] Simone Schnall, Kent D. Harber, Jeanine K. Stefanucci, Dennis R. Proffitt, Social support and the perception of geographical slant, Journal of Experimental Social Psychology, Volume 44, Issue 5, September 2008, Pages 1246-1255.

of the relationship increases. A student who has support and love from parents at home, positive supportive friends, and a nurturing school environment has the key essentials to dare greatly in life. Students who are missing these things see a much steeper hill in front of them. They may even start the journey up the hill, but it is much easier to stop and turn back if the essential element of positive connection is not present.

Leo Buscaglia told a story, actually many stories, that reinforced this point.

A little girl and her father were crossing a bridge. The father was kind of scared so he asked his little daughter, "Sweetheart, please hold my hand so that you don't fall into the river."

The little girl said, "No, Dad. You hold my hand."

"What's the difference?" asked the puzzled father.

"There's a big difference," replied the little girl.

"If I hold your hand and something happens to me, chances are that I may let your hand go. But if you hold my hand, I know for sure that no matter what happens, you will never let my hand go."

In any relationship, the essence of trust is not in its bind, but in its bond. This requires us to hold the hand of the person who loves you rather than expecting them to hold yours. If both have that mindset, the bond is as strong as it can be.

This is a simple lesson that we learned the first time we played "Red Rover" when we were kids. We looked for someone who would hold our hands tightly. No one was breaking through our hand held chain link! On the other hand, if you were called out to run across and try to break through the human chain, you were looking for the weakest link … the two who likely did not have the bond that could hold through the extreme pressure of you running full blast into their linked hands.

Life tends to break though weak links. Strengthening the bond with our students and helping them create bonds with people that will "hold their hand" right back is a task we have to continually take on for our kids. It is also a task that we will benefit greatly from if we would do the same for ourselves.

Check out the Chapter 9 "Post Chapter Video" on You Tube at the following:

http://youtu.be/TmVzGlb9FR0

Chapter 10 - The Joy of the Journey

There's nothing like the feeling that you're really wanted! – Charlie Brown

"Joy is a sustained sense of well-being and internal peace - a connection to what matters." - Oprah

"Grief can take care of itself, but to get the full value of a joy you must have somebody to divide it with." – Mark Twain

I love the response that I saw on the Internet the other day when a child was asked what he wanted to be when he grew up. The child's response was "Happy!" As a parent of four sons and a man that strives to live life to the fullest, I love the answer. It is exactly what I want for my family, my staff, my students, and myself. Working to that end is a challenge, and there seems to be a myriad of ideas and concepts on what "happiness" is. I'll get to some thoughts on happiness as we journey through this chapter.

It hit me that for many of our kids, joy and happiness are out there, but their current journey through life looks very different. I can see it in many of their faces and the whole aura they emit.

Recently I was given an amazing moment of clarity concerning my dad. I feel it was a gift from God for me to use when I work with kids or other adults that work with kids. I was allowed to feel the overwhelming sadness of an orphaned child on one of the worst days of his life. While painful, it has served to soften my heart even more to the pain that many children experience—often in silence.

Dad was an amazing man. He was basically orphaned at the age of six. His mom died of tuberculosis, and his dad, a truck driver, had little interest in the three sons she left behind so they were farmed out and passed around to different relatives who didn't really want them either. Dad ended up in the home of his Aunt Lucille.

When I was young, I got to experience this woman who really cared about me and loved me. As I grew older, I realized this was probably compensation for how horrid she treated my Dad. His days living with her consisted of coming home from school and immediately going out to help dig the new sewers that were being put into the town of Madison, Kansas or doing cleaning work in the house. In the house, he had to get on his hands and knees and scrub the floors with a rag. When he was not doing it to her satisfaction, she would hit him in the head hard with the wooden handle of a hammer. He would then be fed supper and have to do the dishes. He was then instructed to do his homework and practice the one activity he was allowed to do—play his baritone. Dad was not allowed to participate in sports or activities because, as his Aunt Lucille clearly stated, they were foolishness. His relief from this was bedtime. This was his daily cycle.

Occasionally he would have a different type of work to do. At the age of 10, he was working out on an oil pump that needed serviced. Oil pumps are by design extremely heavy. One of these heavy parts swung around and crushed my Dad's toes on his right foot. He was taken from the field to the wood loading dock of the train depot/ice house. His Uncle Wilbur worked there. He sat there while they tried to figure out what to do. They took him to the doctor, and he sat there the entire day until the doctor agreed to see him. By that time it was too late. The toes were turning black and would have to be cut off.

This past year I took my son, Tanner, to begin his freshman year of college. By coincidence, Tanner looks more like my Dad than any other of my sons. After we got Tanner situated in Manhattan, we decided to take a different route home that would take us by the town of Madison, Kansas. Madison sits at the bottom and on the east side of a huge hill. At the bottom of the hill is where my Dad's Aunt Lucille and Uncle Wilbur lived. It is where Dad lived at the age of 10. We drove by the house. It was abandoned, falling apart, and overgrown with weeds. We drove on to the edge of town where the Depot/Ice House stood.

I pulled up in front of the Depot/Ice House and told my wife the story. I've told this story many,

many times, but this time was different. Even now I find writing about it impossible to do without tears. At that moment I was given the gift of feeling part of what my Dad felt as he sat there with crushed toes. Not only did he have crushed, bloody toes, but he was alone.

There were others who carried him to the dock so that someone else could do something with him, but he knew at the age of 10 that he was alone. The physical pain was immense, but nothing compared to the deep sadness of realizing no one cared for him. No one was going to push a doctor to see him immediately. He was going to get the least. He hungered for a Mom who would wrap him in her arms and whisper in his ear that it was going to be OK. He hungered for a Dad who would carry him to the car to be taken to a doctor and demand treatment … NOW. He knew he was getting none of that. He hungered for love that was nowhere to be found.

I sat there and fought back the tears of lament for this 10-year old boy who would become my dad. I'm sure my wife would think I was crazy if I just broke down, so I refrained. It is a miracle that my Dad did not die of Erasmus—the disease orphans die of on a regular basis when they receive no love, no holding, and no hugging. The basics of food, water, and clothing are not enough. They simply turn their head to the wall and die. It is a miracle that he survived the journey through this sadness, this lament, to become the amazing Dad who loved his kids more than life and showed that through the gift of his time playing with them and supporting them.

I wish I had been there to hug that little 10-year-old boy and whisper in his ear that it was going to be all right. I wish I had been there to fight the good fight for the needs of this 10-year-old orphan so that his needs would be met on that terrible day. That is impossible, but instead I will be the one who will love other children who are orphaned or living basically as orphans even if they still have parents. I do this because it is right, and I do this to honor the lament of the 10-year-old orphan, who would become my Dad, sitting there on the wood loading dock of the Depot/Ice House in Madison, Kansas in 1946.

Escaping from horrific sadness that permeates the lives of so many of our kids requires help. It requires us to love them unconditionally … vulnerably. Finding the road to happiness is seemingly impossible for those on the journey of loneliness and sadness. There are so many obstacles that can get in our way when we try to change the road we travel.

There are so many books in print that explain to us what happiness is, how to be happy, how to lead a happy life, how to make others happy, etc.… Many are contradictory; many offer great advice; and some can even prove to be detrimental. If one were to try "how to be happy" from a book, one would want to sift through the written advice carefully. One thing that we do know as a result of recent research and from natural law, connection to others seems to bring about a sense of happiness in people.

Little kids who spend the majority of their time at home are surrounded by the only reality they know. Whether they are raised in poverty or in the lap of luxury, they only really know one reality. And then they go to school.

At first young students don't notice differences among themselves. They are enamored by all that school is and most are enamored with their teacher (assuming they have a teacher who is remotely effective). As the years pass, they start to notice that they are wearing different clothes or have different experiences. Spring break happens and many of our kids in poverty are not really sure where their meals are going to come from that week while other classmates may be going on great family vacations. Spring break, Christmas break, summer break ends and they come back to share their experiences.

You may have been one of these children in poverty who suddenly realized that there is a different reality than the one in which you live. I've watched it happen. The sadness that happens often turns to anger. We know that the weeks before Christmas break and after are tough for so many kids. They live in a country where joy is often based on things, and when many don't have the basics, we have a tough job engaging them so that we can fight the inherit sadness that begins to show through. Our culture in the United States makes this difficult. It reminds me of a great study that shed some light on joy and happiness.

It seems that those who measure happiness point out that some of the poorest nations consistently rank higher in happiness than those who live in the wealthiest of nations. Oliver Burkman, in his book "The Antidote," looked at happiness from a different angle that took direct shots at those who profess that simply thinking positive thoughts can bring happiness. While doing this, he ran across a study of a Kenyan township in Kibera, which is just outside of Nairobi.

These people live in what we would call deep poverty and live in such fragile conditions that they constantly have to face the very fundamental insecurity of their existence. They have no belief that they are suddenly going to run into a bunch of money, get a promotion at work, or get a raise that will propel them into a big house with financial security that will make them happy. "Insecurity" is a given for them. They are forced to find ways to live with this insecurity of life.

These Kiberan tribes people are some of the happiest people on earth, and they come by this by building strong relationships with family and neighbors. It is as simple as that. They realize that death and disease is a very real force, but in the interim, they will build connections to find joy.[11] "Stuff" or money will never be an option. All they have is each other, and they celebrate in one another. Not such a bad thing.

Now it is true that money can make things easier—to a point. Princeton recently conducted a study that looked at "overall satisfaction in life." For the sake of argument, let's call that "happiness." They discovered that money did help with happiness up to a point and that point was a $75,000 salary per year. After that, additional money did not help with feelings of satisfaction or happiness at all. More money does not make happiness. Connection seems to breed happiness.

Most of us want our own kids and our students to experience joy in life. Not long ago a team of psychologists performed a series of studies that definitely suggest that the act of sharing your good news multiplies its benefits for your happiness and longer-term life satisfaction. What they discovered is that sharing stories of positive experiences with others in a way that goes beyond just talking with a friend or just recalling a positive experience with a friend creates happiness. The researchers recorded the mood of students after

[11] Burkeman, Oliver (2012). "The Antidote.: Happiness for People Who Can't Stand Positive Thinking." Faber & Faber, New York, NY.

they had written about a positive experience or just shared neutral information with a friend. They discovered that sharing your good news with another person is beneficial in bringing feelings of joy.

They also discovered that these feelings of joy are not fleeting. Part of their research stretched the study out over four weeks with the use of diaries. Those who shared the positive experience twice or more in a week were happier and more satisfied with life than those who just wrote about what they had learned in class that week or just shared basic information.

Here is the most revealing part of the study. When one shares his or her good news, the amplification of joy is not guaranteed. The friend, relative, or partner who is receiving your good news has a very important role to play. They have to respond in what the researchers called "active-constructive" style.

The study had stories shared with others through e-mails and they received responses in four different ways:
1. "Active Consideration" (Super job! Amazing work! I'm so proud of you!)
2. "Active Destruction" (No biggy…doesn't sound that hard to me.)
3. "Passive Construction" (Nothing more than just a smiley face symbol.)

4. "Passive Destruction"   (Yeah, someone already told me that.)

Those who received "Active Consideration" reported receiving twice as much joy as those who received any of the other three types of feedback. When I think of the teachers who have such amazing power to facilitate joy and happiness, or not, I can't help but wonder about the impact on learning that teachers have.

So the joy of the journey seems to have much more to do with who you are on the journey with than the road you happen to be on. It is still a great idea to help kids get on a road that will more easily lead to joy and happiness, but it is much more important to come along with our kids on the journey and support them with "Active Consideration." Oh, let's just call it what it is … love.

Heart to Heart Teaching—teaching from the heart to the heart—gives us our best shot to positively impact our students, strengthen learning, brighten our world and the students' world, and to leave an enduring legacy that will live on long after we have departed this earth.

Check out the Chapter 10 "Post Chapter Video" on You Tube at the following:

http://youtu.be/4RvbRZY6YF8

Acknowledgments

Kellie – Thank you for your unwavering love and support and making me believe…

Stephen, Jake, Tanner & Chris – Thank you for your love and for believing I am better than I am.

Dad and Mom (Bob and Eda Woolf) – Thank you for loving me and helping me to believe I can do anything or be anything.

The K-12 Teachers Who Taught Me – Thank you for helping to mold my heart and dreams. Thank you for developing my bag of tools.

The Hero Educators I Have Served With In My Career – Thank you for inspiring me in a wide variety of ways to make a difference and for the difference you make or made in the lives of our kids.

Dr. George Crawford, Dr. Mike Neal, Dr. Andy Tompkins, Dr. Kent Stewart – Thank you for being amazing educators that prepared me and hundreds of others to be leaders in education and in life. Thank you for instilling in me a belief I can make a difference!

Louise Bevilacqua, Marlon Towse, Randy Clark, Coach Mike Neal, Paul Biays, Rick Beeler, Paul Kukula, Larry Krebbs, Sharon DeBusk, Colleen Guy, Chuck Sodergren, and Dad (Robert Woolf) – Thank you for being amazing, special educators in my life and who I modelled my life after. Please know you are loved by me and thousands of others.

Jostens Renaissance and the Amazing Renaissance Leaders, Larry Biddle, Clint Jones, Charley Nelson, Richard Parkhouse and Many More – Thank you for being passionate about kids and educators and for building and supporting a way of living as an educator that rewards, recognizes, respects, and reinforces the amazing things we want for our kids and "staffulty." Thank you for believing in me and giving me a voice.

Angela Maiers – Thank you for being an amazing passionate educator and for being a moral support for the kinds of differences we are trying to make in the lives of our kids.

Dr. George Crawford and Dr. Mike Neal – Thank you for being my cheerleader and making me believe I can do it. In fact, now that my Dad is gone from this earth, it is you that I want to make proud.

Dr. Michelle Carney-Ray, Dwight Carter, Dr. Crawford, and Dr. Neal – Thank you for being a part of this book and supporting "Heart 2 Heart Teaching" as well as being "Heart 2 Heart Educators" in your own right.

Kevin Honeycutt, Ginger Lewman, Jim Beeghley, and Cody Heitschmidt – Thank you for believing in my message and working to get the message of being a passionate, "Heart 2 Heart Educator" out to as many people as possible.

Kay Tibbs and George Crawford – Thank you for reading through my writing, editing, and speaking the truth with kindness as I developed this heartfelt message.

Terri Peckham, Lori Blaine, and Cody Heitschmidt – Thank you and the whole ESSDACK Team for making this book possible!

Tanner Woolf, Kellie Woolf, Taylor Lambin, Abby Vogts, and Lorena South – Thank you for all of the filming (Tanner and Kellie), tech help (Taylor), picture taking for the cover (Abby), and for being the student model (Lorena). I could not have finished this labour of love without you.

Bibliography

As The Planes Turn (2009). "Southwest Airlines "Malice in Dallas" Part Five. March 20, 1992. **http://www.youtube.com/watch?v=H_sXAdUNF nc**

Baby Mama (2008). **https://www.youtube.com/watch?v=IMSd1lbxm FA**.

Brown, Brene' (2013). "Oprah's Life Class: Part 1," OWN.

Burkeman, Oliver (2012). "The Antidote.: Happiness for People Who Can't Stand Positive Thinking." Faber & Faber, New York, NY.

Comer, James (2005). "Leave No Child Behind: Preparing Today's Youth For Tomorrow's World," Yale University Press: New Haven and London.

Connelly, Michael F. & Clandinin, D. Jean (1990). "Stories of Experience and Narrative Inquiry." Educational Researcher, Vol. 19, No. 5, (Jun.-Jul., 1990). pp. 2-14.

Craik, F.I.M., & McDowd, J.M. (1987). Age-differences in recall and recognition. *Journal of*

Experimental Psychology: Learning, Memory and Cognition, 13, pp. 474-479.

Fitzgerald, Paul (2009). BreakThrough, Heart Connexion Seminars,
http://www.heartconnexion.org/index.html

Frankl, Viktor (1959). "Man's Search For Meaning," Beacon Press: Boston, MA.

Hattie, John (2009). "Visible Learning; a synthesis of over 800 meta-analyses relating to achievement." London; Routledge.

Payne, Ruby (1995). *"A Framework For Understanding Poverty."* Baytown, TX. RFT.

Simone Schnall, Kent D. Harber, Jeanine K. Stefanucci, Dennis R. Proffitt (2008). "Social support and the perception of geographical slant", Journal of Experimental Social Psychology, Volume 44, Issue 5, September 2008, pp. 1246-1255.

Made in the USA
Monee, IL
25 August 2022

12561399R00069